365

Fascinating

FACTS

about

ISRAEL

365

Fascinating

FACTS

about

ISRAEL

CLARENCE WAGNER

First printing: October 2006

ISBN-13: 978-0-89221-667-3
ISBN-10: 0-89221-667-0
Library of Congress Catalog Number: 99-069281

Previously published under the title *365 Fascinating Facts about the Holy Land.*

All Scripture is from the New International Version of the Bible unless otherwise noted.

Printed in the United States of America.

Please visit our website for other great titles:
www.newleafpress.net.

For information regarding author interviews, please contact the publicity department at (870) 438-5288.

New Leaf Press
A Division of New Leaf Publishing Group

This book is dedicated to my family
and my faithful ministry staff
who support and sojourn with me in the land of Israel
as I pursue God's high calling
to reunite the Church
with God's destiny for Israel and the Jewish people.

CONTENTS

Introduction 9

1. The Location of the Land 13

2. The Glory of All Lands 21

3. Covenants and the Land and People 52

4. Jerusalem 86

5. Israel in Prophecy 121

6. History and Israel Today 151

   Endnotes 210

   Bibliography 212

   About the Author 215

Introduction

God has blessed me with the privilege of living in Israel — my home for over 30 years.

As I travel the world speaking about Israel, I often hear many of the same questions over and over again. Whether it is in South Africa or Canada, Australia or Brazil, the UK or the USA, one thing that Christians want to have is a summary of the key Scriptures about Israel, Jerusalem, the Jewish people, Bible prophecy, and how they all relate to the Church. God has much to say about His covenant people and His land, Israel, as well as how His church should relate to both.

That is the subject of this book. You will find it an easy-to-use reference with one key fact for every day of the year, or you can read them all at once. This is a very relevant and important biblical subject, given the prophetic day in which we live when all eyes are on Israel as we await the soon coming of the Lord.

The land of Israel is the only place on earth which God says He owns. Of course, we know the whole world is His, yet this one parcel of land on the earth has a unique relationship to Him. About Israel, He says, "The land must not be sold permanently, because the land is mine and you are but aliens and my tenants" (Lev. 25:23).

God gave His land to Abraham and his descendants (the Jewish people) in an unconditional covenant. God said: "I will establish my covenant as an everlasting covenant between me and you and your descendants after you for the generations to come, to be your God and the God of your descendants after you. The whole land of Canaan, where you are now an alien, I will give as an everlasting possession to you and your descendants after you; and I will be their God" (Gen. 17:7–8).

The Jewish people were a chosen people for three purposes: to worship God in this land and show the world the blessing of serving the one true God of the universe; to receive, record, and transmit the Word of God (through them we have our Bible); and finally, to be the human channel for the Messiah, from whom we have our salvation. These people are so special to God that He called them "my people" (Exod. 3:7, 10:3).

By the blood of Christ, the church of Jesus Christ receives its atonement and salvation, plus an additional bonus. The blood of Christ makes us a part of the covenants God made with the Jewish people, the descendants of Abraham, Isaac, and Jacob, concerning the land of Israel and the promises He made to them. Ephesians 2:12–13 says, "Remember that at that time you were separate from Christ, excluded from citizenship in Israel and foreigners to the covenants of the promise, without hope and without God in the world. But now in Christ Jesus you who once were far away have been brought near through the blood of Christ."

In a day when the whole world is focusing on the Middle East and the modern state of Israel, exactly what does the Bible say about God's parcel of land, and who has a right to it?

When we come to the modern-day Israel-Palestine issue, people often ask the question, "Just what right do Israel and the Jewish people have to this land?" Arguments are continually brought forth concerning the rights of the Palestinians and the rights of the Israelis that seem logical to the people who present them. But a basic question still remains in my mind as I listen to the many conflicting viewpoints concerning this parcel of land: "Who has the ultimate authority to determine rights concerning this special piece of real estate?"

The biblical answer to this question is that God alone determines the "rights" that any of us have. Something is right or wrong because of divine decree, not human feeling or human reason. The existence of God previous to the creation of the universe and mankind gives Him the right to determine our "rights." Morality exists because God exists. Authority exists because God exists, and Almighty God has already determined the rights of the Jewish people to Israel, the land God owns and has deeded over to them. It is the responsibility of the Church to understand God's Word on this subject and uphold it.

As Christians, we are not to be swayed "to and fro, and carried about with every wind of doctrine" (Eph. 4:14; KJV). This is true for all scriptural teaching, including what God has to say about the land of Israel, the people He chose to possess it, and why. Let us look together at *365 Fascinating Facts about Israel.*

CHAPTER ONE

THE LOCATION
OF THE LAND

1

The land of the Bible has been called by many names: Canaan, the Land of Milk and Honey, the Promised Land, Israel, Judah, Idumea, and Palestine. From the Scriptures, we also know the names of its regions, either as the tribal areas given by God to the 12 tribes of Israel (Josh. 13–21), or by its geographical names, e.g., Judea, Samaria, Galilee, the Shephelah (the coastal plains), the Arava, the Negev, etc. Today, the modern state of Israel possesses much of these regions, yet only a portion of the larger ancient land promised by God.

In the Bible, we find other more descriptive or poetic names given to this same land: Beulah (Isa. 62:4), the holy land (Zech. 2:12), Immanuel's land (Isa. 8:8), Jeshurun (Deut. 33:26; Isa. 44:2), land of the Hebrews (Gen. 40:15), country of the Jews (Acts 10:39), pleasant land (Dan. 8:9; Zech 7:14; KJV), goodly mountain (Deut. 3:25; KJV), and the Lord's land (Hos. 9:3).[1]

God chose this specific land for himself for a purpose. God owns the land. The land of Israel is the only place on earth, which God says He owns in terms of property ownership, that can be transferred. Of course, we know the whole world is His, as the Psalmist says, "The earth is the LORD's, and everything in it, the world, and all who live in it" (Ps. 24:1).

2

However, there is one parcel of land on the earth that has a unique relationship to Him. About Israel, He says,

"The land must not be sold permanently, because the land is mine and you are but aliens and my tenants" (Lev. 25:23). In fact, there are numerous references to Israel being "God's Land." In Jeremiah, God calls it "my land" (Jer. 2:7).

Through Isaiah, God speaks about defending His land when He says, "I will crush the Assyrian in my land; on my mountains I will trample him down" (Isa. 14:25). Even when speaking of a prophetic day to come, God still calls Israel His land. Through Ezekiel, He says, "In days to come, O Gog, I will bring you against my land, so that the nations may know me when I show myself holy through you before their eyes" (Ezek. 38:16).

3   God loves His land and cares for it. Read what Moses had to say about God's love for the Promised Land: "It is a land the LORD your God cares for; the eyes of the LORD your God are continually on it from the beginning of the year to its end" (Deut. 11:12).

Without telling Abraham where he was going, God called Abraham to a specific place for a specific purpose. In Genesis 12:1–3, we read, "The LORD had said to Abram, 'Leave your country, your people and your father's household and go to the land I will show you. I will make you into a great nation and I will bless you; I will make your name great, and you will be a blessing. I will bless those who bless you, and whoever curses you I will curse; and all the peoples on earth will be blessed through you.' " In short, God had a plan (the salvation of the world), so He chose a particular man (Abraham) and took Him to a specific land (the land of Canaan, later renamed Israel by God).

5  So where is this land? The land God gave in an everlasting covenant to Abraham and his descendants was the "whole land of Canaan," located in the same region where we find the modern state of Israel today. "The Canaanites were in the land. The LORD appeared to Abram and said, 'To your offspring, I will give this land' " (Gen. 12:6–7). Genesis 17:7–8 states: "I will establish my covenant as an everlasting covenant between me and you and your descendants after you for the generations to come, to be your God and the God of your descendants after you. The whole land of Canaan, where you are now an alien, I will give as an everlasting possession to you and your descendants after you; and I will be their God."

God promised Abraham and his descendants a land much bigger than has ever been conquered by the Israelites of old, even under the great empire of Solomon or the Israelis today. "He [God] also said to him [Abram], 'I am the LORD, who brought you out of Ur of the Chaldeans to give you this land to take possession of it' " (Gen. 15:7). "On that day, the Lord made a covenant with Abram and said, 'To your descendants I give this land, from the river of Egypt to the great river, the Euphrates — the land of the Kenites, Kenizzites, Kadmonites, Hittites, Perizzites, Rephaites, Amorites, Canaanites, Girgashites and Jebusites' " (Gen. 15:18–21; compare Josh. 1:4). A much more detailed description of this territory can be found in Numbers 34:1–12. This region included all of the area in the land of Israel today, plus all of Jordan, Lebanon, and much of Syria.

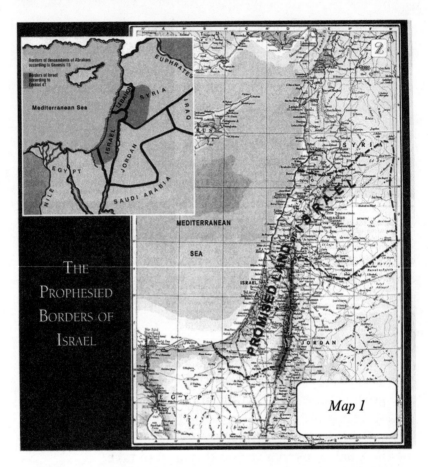

THE PROPHESIED BORDERS OF ISRAEL

Map 1

7

It is clear from the descriptions of the land that God gave to Abraham and his descendants as an everlasting possession that other tribes lived in this land. Nevertheless, since God owns the land, He can decide whom to give it to, so as to accomplish His redemptive purposes on earth. Therefore, when God called Abraham to create a new nation of people to live in "His land," it was God who started what I call the "musical chair" game of Middle East nations. In other words, by establishing the Israelites in a region of other peoples, and then telling Israel to push these pagan tribes out of the

Promised Land, a continuous cycle of dispossessed peoples, looking for a new land in which to live, was begun.

Thus, even today, the Middle East always seems to be one or two nations short. Often two or more competing groups are trying to claim the same land, e.g., Israel and the Palestinians, Israel and the Syrians, the Kurds, Turkey and Iraq, etc. In Israel's case, claims can be put forth, but they will not prosper unless they line up with God's plan for His land and His people.

Within the larger land area promised to the Children of Abraham, the provincial borders of the tribal land were also described by God to the sons of Jacob, the tribes of Israel. So detailed is the description down to the most minute detail in the Book of Joshua, chapters 13–21, that even today you can take a modern map of Israel and draw these borders along the rivers, valleys, hilltops, and cities, just as it is written. Unlike today's smaller borders of Israel, these tribal areas extended on both the eastern and western side of the Jordan River, and into what today is southern Lebanon and part of southwest Syria (see Map 2).

Regardless of the size of Israel during different periods in history, the portion of the land consistently inhabited by the Israelites was referred to as being "from Dan to Beersheva." Dan is the tribal area at the northern end of the Hulah Valley north of the Sea of Galilee at the foot of Mount Hermon and the sources of the Jordan River. Beersheva is a southern city in the Negev Desert where Abraham lived for some time, having made a treaty with Abimelech (Gen. 21:22–32). It is on the edge of the driest part of the desert farther south,

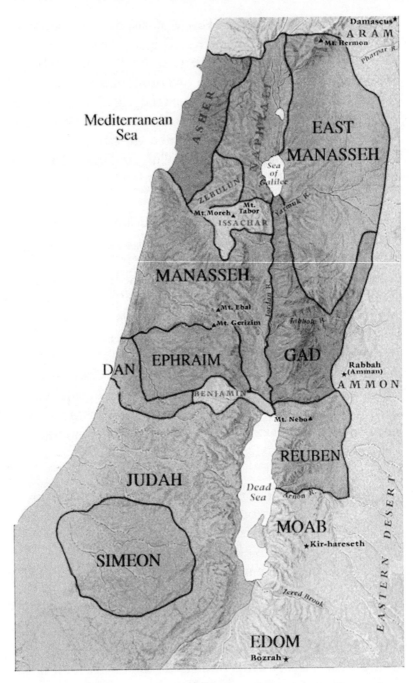

Map 2

and marked the end of the easily inhabitable land in the days of the Bible. Between these two points is a mere 140 miles (225 km). Compared with the rich Nile Delta in Egypt or the fertile fields of Mesopotamia between the Tigris and Euphrates Rivers, the land of Israel is relatively poor and small. The size of Israel, for much of the biblical period and even now, is the size of the state of New Jersey in the USA, yet this little land has figured prominently in the affairs of the world, and its own stormy history provides much evidence for its vital significance and importance.[2]

Today, when we look at a map, we are taught in school to view the world with all the countries lined up north to south, where a right direction would be east and a left direction would be west.

This is not the case in the Bible. God and the Bible's orientation toward the land of the Bible (Israel) is as though He were viewing it from heaven, from over the Mediterranean Sea looking east. The directions in the Bible of going left and right correspond with north and south, not west and east (see Map 3). Yemen, for example, a country at the southern tip of the Saudi Arabian peninsula, is a name that means, in Hebrew, "right." It is the farthest country to the right, or south, of Israel.

To illustrate this point, let's look at Genesis: "The LORD said to Abram after Lot had parted from him, 'Lift up your eyes from where you are and look north and south, east and west. All the land that you see I will give to you and your offspring for ever. I will make your offspring like the dust of the earth, so that if anyone could count the dust, then your offspring could be counted. Go, walk through the length and breadth of the land, for I am giving it to you' " (Gen. 13:14–17).

In verse 14, the directions of north, south, east, and west are written in Hebrew, as follows: *tzafona, negbah, kedemah,* and *yamah.* What do they mean literally? *Tzafona* means "toward the north;" *negbah* means "toward the Negev," which is the southernmost region of Israel; *kedemah* means "forward," (e.g., an Israeli army officer will say to his troops, *kedemah,* and then lead them forward to the front lines); and *yamah* means "toward the sea," i.e., the Mediterranean Sea. From this, you can see God looked east across the land, as *kedemah* (forward) is translated east, *yamah* (toward the sea) is west, and *negbah* (a region to His right) is translated south.

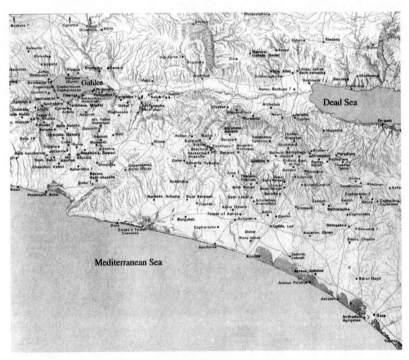

Map 3

CHAPTER TWO

THE GLORY OF ALL LANDS

11   The land of the Bible was also known as "the land of milk and honey." In Exodus 3:8, God said to Moses, "So I have come down to rescue them from the hand of the Egyptians and to bring them up out of that land into a good and spacious land, a land flowing with milk and honey — the home of the Canaanites, Hittites, Amorites, Perizzites, Hivites and Jebusites." Through Ezekiel, God was recounting this conversation and said, "On that day I sware unto them, to bring them forth out of the land of Egypt into a land that I had searched out for them, flowing with milk and honey . . . the glory of all lands" (Ezek. 20:6; ASV).

The land of milk and honey refers to the fact   12
that the land could support animals that provide
milk and cheese, e.g., sheep, goats, camels, and
eventually cattle, as well as flowering fruit trees
that provided nectar for bees and fruit for jam.
Animals and trees also meant there would be
water. The promise of a land of milk and honey
confirmed God's blessing for the Israelites, considering the entire region is mostly arid desert.

13    Here is how Moses described the blessed-ness of this land to the Children of Israel: "Observe the commands of the LORD your God, walking in his ways and revering him. For the LORD your God is bringing you into a good land — a land with streams and pools of water,

with springs flowing in the valleys and hills; a land with wheat and barley, vines and fig-trees, pomegranates, olive oil and honey; a land where bread will not be scarce and you will lack nothing; a land where the rocks are iron and you can dig copper out of the hills" (Deut. 8:6–9).

The 12 men that Moses sent in to explore the Promised Land came back with a huge cluster of grapes from the Valley of Eshcol, along with pomegranates and figs (Num. 13:23) and gave this report: "We went into the land to which you sent us, and it does flow with milk and honey! Here is its fruit" (Num. 13:27).

14

15

The "glory of all lands" (Ezek. 20:6) can refer to the fact that God sees Israel as His land (Lev. 25:23) and, therefore, it is the number one nation of the world, both spiritually and literally. However, in connection with the term, "a land flowing with milk and honey," it could also have a more temporal connotation.

Living in Israel for these many years, it is easy for me to see that the terrain, flora, and fauna of this land reflects all of the surrounding continents: Eurasia to the north, Asia to the east, Africa to the south, and the Mediterranean basin to the west, all of which cross-sect in the land of Israel. Israel is like a connecting hinge between these continental spheres of influence.

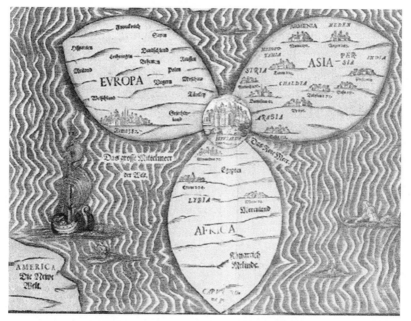

Map 4. Helmstadt, 1581, woodcut

16

In general terms, Israel is a mountainous land. Running through this land of the Bible is a deep gash in the earth. In Israel, it is called the Jordan Valley (north of the Dead Sea) and Arava Valley (south of the Dead Sea). They are the same valley and are part of the great Syrian-African rift valley. It extends over 4,000 miles (6,437 km) from the mountains of Turkey through Syria, the Beka'a valley of Lebanon, the Jordan and Arava Valleys in Israel, the Red Sea, and then into Africa, going as far south as Tanzania.

17

At the Sea of Galilee, the Jordan Valley is 656 feet (200 m) below sea level, and at the Dead Sea it drops to 1,312 feet (400 m) below sea level — the lowest point on earth!

18

The Sea of Galilee is a beautiful freshwater lake that is fed from winter rain run-off from the mountains of Galilee on the west and the Golan Heights on the east. It is 695 feet (212 m) below sea level, 5 miles (8 km) wide, and 13 miles (21 km) long. It is the main water reservoir of Israel and also provides water to Jordan and the Palestinian Authority areas.

The Hebrew name for the Sea of Galilee is Kinneret, which means "harp." This is because the shape of the sea is like the ancient harps, such as those played by King David in the days of the Bible.

The Sea of Galilee.

The Dead Sea is 48 miles (78 km) long and 11 miles (18 km) wide at its widest point. Its depth is 1,007 feet (307 m), making this the deepest natural fissure on the earth's surface. The Dead Sea is dead because it is so salty: 25 percent of the water's content is salt.

19

The water is clear, yet is bitter and nauseous to taste because of the magnesium chloride and smooth and oily to the touch because of the calcium chloride.

20   The salts in the Dead Sea are worth trillions of dollars in value and are a prize as valuable as any oil field! These riches, mined by the Dead Sea Works at Sedom on the southern end of the sea, are used for fertilizers and other chemical uses. They include: 22,000,000,000 tons of magnesium chloride, 11,000,000,000 of sodium chloride, 7,000,000,000 of calcium chloride, 2,000,000,000 of potassium chloride, and 1,000,000,000 of magnesium bromide.[1]

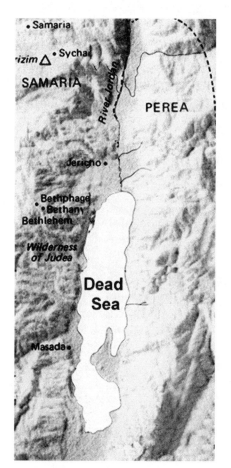

Map 5

Could this be part of the riches and plunder that will attract the armies of Gog in an invasion of Israel in a day yet to come, mentioned in the Book of Ezekiel? In this passage, Gog plans to invade Israel in a prophetic day, like today, when it is a "land of unwalled villages" and attack "a peaceful and unsuspecting people — all of them living without walls and without gates and bars" (Ezek. 38:11). Gog is asked the question, "Have you come to plunder? Have you gathered your hordes to loot, to carry off silver and gold, to take away livestock and goods and to seize much plunder?" (Ezek. 38:13).

The ancients called the Dead Sea, "the Salt Sea" (Gen. 14:3; Deut. 3:17; Num. 34:3). By the time of the Romans, they called it by a Latin name, the *Lacus Asphaltitis* (the Asphalt Lake), because huge lumps of petroleum-rich asphalt and bitumen would float up from the bottom of the sea. It was harvested for fuel and exported to surrounding countries.

21

The Dead Sea Valley, also called the Vale of Siddim, was known as early as the time of Abraham as a source of this fuel and is mentioned in Genesis, "Now the Valley of Siddim was full of tar pits" (Gen. 14:10).

The first century Jewish historian, Flavius Josephus (A.D. 37–93), described the Dead Sea (Lacus Asphaltitis): "However, it casts up black clods of bitumen in many parts of it, these swim at the top of the water, and resemble both in shape and bigness headless bulls; and when the laborers that belong to the lake come to it, and catch hold of it as it hangs together, they draw it into their ships. . . . This bitumen is not only useful for the caulking of ships, but for cure of man's body, accordingly it is mixed in a great many medicines."[2]

Even today, oil seeps from the ground in areas around the southern end of the Dead Sea, and a Christian oil exploration company from Texas holds the rights to drill for oil.

Salt columns in the Dead Sea

22

The Dead Sea is so salty partly because of the high evaporation rate. The tons of water that flow into the sea from the surrounding region are loaded with dissolved salts. Being in the middle of the desert, the evaporation rate is phenomenally high (about 5 feet per year), leaving behind the transported dissolved salts.

Because the fresh water of the Jordan River is diverted for farming, the surface level of the Dead Sea has dropped 33 feet (10 m) since 1960.[3] In the 1870s, the British Exploration Society placed a watermark from a boat along a cliff face near Ein Freshka. Today that watermark is 13 feet (4 m) above the present modern road that runs north-south along the Israeli side of the Dead Sea.

The Dead Sea is also salty because there is   23
no outlet. It only receives water that evaporates
in the desert climate.

The Sea of Galilee is sweet because it has
an inflow of water and also an outflow. Therefore, it has been said that the reason the Sea of
Galilee is sweet is because it receives and gives,
while the Dead Sea is dead because it only
receives and never gives. It may be full of riches, but there is no life in it. This is a spiritual lesson for all of us.

24

Another great valley of Israel is the Valley of Armageddon. It gets this name from Revelation 16:16 as the site of the last great battle between the nations of the world and the Lord himself. When Napoleon conquered this region in 1799, he assessed this valley as the greatest arena for a battle to be found anywhere in the world. This is because it is ringed by mountains and has entrances at all four compass points.[4]

This valley is also known by its topographical name, the Valley of Esdraelon, or by names connected with two major cities on the southern edge of this valley, the Valley of Megiddo or the Jezreel Valley. The valley separates the regional areas of Galilee in the north from the mountains of Samaria and the coastal plains along the Mediterranean Sea to the south.

The Valley of Armageddon is shaped like an arrowhead pointing to the Mediterranean coastal city of Haifa. The Beit Shean Valley is the long shaft of the arrow, which extends into the Jordan Valley. Because of the ease of travel through these valleys, the great trade routes of the Middle East were found here.

25

26

One of those routes was "the Way of the Sea" (Isa. 9:1), which the Romans called the Via Maris (see Map 6). It connected Mesopotamia and Europe in the north to Egypt and Africa to the south, so it was a major trading route. From Damascus, the route led southwest to Hazor, through Galilee into the Valley of Megiddo to the coastal plains along the Mediterranean Sea to Egypt. Leaving south from the Valley of Megiddo along this route, you pass into the Dotan Valley, the scene of Joseph being sold to Midianite traders moving south to Egypt.

Another north-south trading route was called the King's Highway that ran south along the plateau of the mountains east of the Jordan/Arava rift valley, from Damascus into the Saudi Arabian peninsula, the Hejaz, via Rabbath-Ammon, modern-day Amman. Traders coming up with their exotic spices who wanted

27

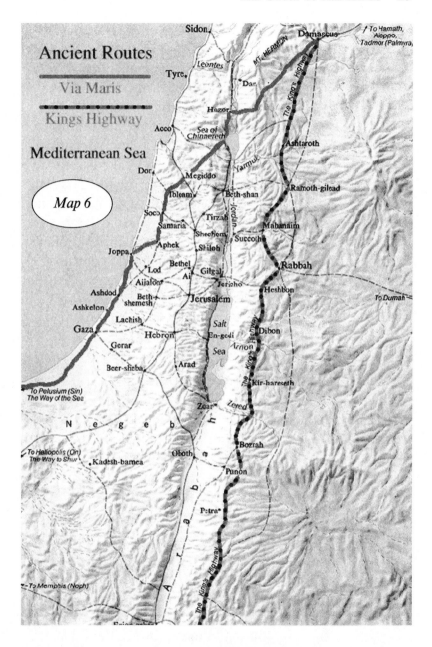

Ancient Routes

Via Maris

Kings Highway

Mediterranean Sea

Map 6

to take their goods to the Mediterranean coast for export would travel on a major east-west trade route via the Beit Shean Valley into the Valley of Megiddo.

28

In a world where most of the trade and travel was by land, control of these vital trade routes made a prime location of its day. Every ambitious ruler aimed to bring these routes within his jurisdiction. Thus, the land of Israel became the occasion of countless military campaigns and historic battles, for whoever held it subject controlled the vital crossroads of the ancient world. Pharaohs of Egypt; kings of Assyria, Babylonia, and Persia; Alexander the Great; Ptolemaic and Seleucid kings; Roman and Byzantine emperors; Arabs; Crusaders; Mamelukes; Turks; and even the British under General Allenby in World War I, all fought for control of this tiny area because the land of Israel was seen as essential to the security and well-being of one side or the other.[5]

West of the Jordan River Valley, the main   29
mountain range starts from Mount Carmel,
southeast along the southern edge of the Valley
of Megiddo, then south through the hill country of Samaria into Judea. These "hills" rise
to a height of 3,000 feet (914 m). Because this
range runs north-south, the corresponding valleys that come off of this range run east-west.
Therefore, the only way to travel north-south is along the
coastal plain in the west, the Jordan Valley in the east, or
right up on top of this range.

30

These mountains are the "mountains of Israel" mentioned in the Bible (Ezek. 6:2–3; 33:28; 36:8, etc.). On this ridge route, we find some famous cities mentioned in the Bible, for example, Shechem, Samaria, Tirza, Jerusalem, Bethlehem, and Hebron. Today, much of this area is in the disputed territories of the West

Bank (biblical Judea and Samaria), which is where most of the stories of the Bible took place and where the Israelites lived for thousands of years. The Palestinian Authority is claiming this land as Arab Muslim territory.

Snow-capped Mount Hermon

31   The highest peak in Israel is Mount Hermon with an altitude of 9,232 feet (2,814 m), which is located in northeast Israel at the north of the Golan Heights. In the Galilee, the highest peak is Mount Meron, rising 3,963 feet (1,208 m). In the south, the Sinai Mountains rise over 7,500 feet (2,286 m). The highest is Mount Catherine at 8,700 feet (2652 m), next to Mount Horeb and Mount Sinai, named after the St. Catherine Monastery which was built to commemorate Moses receiving the Law of God from the Lord on Mount Sinai. East of the Jordan and Arava Valley, the mountains rise to 5,000 feet (1,524 m).[6]

Not only is the Dead Sea mined, but within **32**
the mountains of Israel are minerals that at
times are mentioned in the Bible: phosphates
for fertilizer, uranium, glass sand, kaolin clay,
ochre for red and yellow paints, gypsum, sulfur
— called brimstone in the Bible: "Then the
Lord rained on Sodom and Gomorrah brimstone . . . out of heaven" (Gen. 19:24;NASB).

Also mentioned was bitumen, asphalt, copper, manganese,
feldspar, quartz, pebbles, basalt, marble, granite, and iron
ores: "Iron is taken from the earth, and copper is smelted
from ore" (Job 28:2). Eilat stone is a uniquely beautiful
blue and green stone of gem quality that is used for jewelry.
Most all of these minerals are found in the Negev region.

The copper mines of the Egyptians and King Solomon,
3,000 years old, were found in Timna, along with their
smelting enterprises. Belgian engineers confirmed the presence of 100,000 tons of metallic copper in the mountains
just north of Eilat. In the description of the Promised Land,
Moses confirmed it was "a land where the rocks are iron
and you can dig copper out of the hills" (Deut. 8:9).

33

While the area of much of Israel inhabited
in biblical as well as modern times comprises
only about 8,000 sq. miles, there is an incredible
variety of scenery. Because the mountains rise
just east of the Mediterranean coast and then
drop off below sea level into the Jordan Valley,
the prevailing westerly winds create
a variety of climates and terrain. **34**

Mountains and plains, fertile fields, and
desert are often minutes apart. Israel's width,
from the Mediterranean Sea in the west to the
Dead Sea in the east, is about 50 miles wide

and can be crossed by car in about 90 minutes. Jerusalem, in the Judean Hills, is less than an hour's drive from
Tel Aviv on the coast; and a trip from Metulla, in the far
north, to Eilat at the country's southern tip on the Red
Sea, takes about seven hours by car. The distance from
Jerusalem, at an altitude of 2,739 feet (835 m) above sea
level, to the Dead Sea, which lies about 1,300 feet (400 m)
below sea level, can be driven in less than one hour.[7] In
fact, from my neighborhood in Jerusalem, I can see the
Mediterranean Sea looking west, and the Dead Sea and
the mountains of Moab looking to the east. This is not a
very wide country.

35   There are three basic geographical factors
which have determined the character of Israel:
its setting within the Mediterranean zone, its
position at the crossroads of three continents
and between two oceans (the Indian Ocean
which extends into the Gulf of Eilat and the
Mediterranean Sea), and its situation on the
boundary line between the two extremes of the
arid desert and land that can be sown.[8]

36

Basically, there are two seasons in Israel,
the rainy winter and the hot, dry summer. In
most years, the weather will change from a hot
summer day to a cold winter day overnight
and stay that way until the spring. Then, in the
spring, the weather will be cool and pleasant,
and often in one day, it will become hot and
dry and summer resumes.

Each year, Holland gives thousands of tulip bulbs to the
city of Jerusalem. It invariably is when they are at their peak
blossom that the winter to summer transition takes place in
a day and the delicate petals fall quickly.

37

In general, the average temperatures in Israel range from an average high of 104 degrees F (40°C) in Eilat in August down to an average of 31 degrees F (-1°C) in Safed in the north.

Mount Hermon is colder and not only has snow but also a very respectable ski resort and lift that is enjoyed by many each year. Snow is seen in the mountains of the Golan annually, and in Galilee, Samaria, and Judea (including Jerusalem) about every two to three years.

The highest temperature recorded in Israel was 129.2 degrees F (54°C), measured in the Jordan Valley in 1921.

The land that God was bringing the Hebrews into was a land of rain, unlike their experience in Egypt: " The land you are entering to take over is not like the land of Egypt, from which you have come, where you planted your seed and irrigated it by foot as in a vegetable garden. But the land you are crossing the Jordan to take possession of is a land of mountains and valleys that drinks rain from heaven" (Deut. 11:10–11).

38

The phrase, "irrigated it by foot" is a reference to the way fields are watered in Egypt where the crops are grown along the Nile River and water is taken from the river by means of a water wheel operated with one's foot. In Israel, God would water the fields with rain He would provide.

39

God was the provider of the rain that fell in the land of Israel. This point was made very clearly to the Israelites before they entered into the land: "So if you faithfully obey the commands I am giving you today — to love the LORD your God and to serve him with all your heart and with all your soul — then I will send rain on your land in its season, both autumn and spring rains, so that you may gather in your grain, new wine and oil. I will provide grass in the fields for your cattle, and you will eat and be satisfied" (Deut. 11:13–15).

The rainy season in Israel is between November and February. However, the Bible speaks of the early, or former, rains *(yoreh)* and the latter rains *(malkosh)*. The early rains are the showers that can fall in late September (autumn), and the latter rains are showers that can fall in late March or April (spring). These are always an extra blessing.

40

41

Because of the effect of the central mountain range, the moisture that blows eastward from the Mediterranean Sea is squeezed out of the air like a sponge as it rises over the mountains. However, once the air passes over the central mountain range, where you find Jerusalem, Bethlehem, and Hebron, the air expands as the land sinks below sea level into the Jordan Valley. Just like relaxing the pressure on a sponge, the moisture is no longer released as rain. Consequently, the western slopes of the central mountain range are green and watered from the rain, and the eastern slope is the Judean Desert, where you find Jericho with an average annual rainfall of a mere two inches (5 cm).

During the rainy winter, the rain does not fall evenly, and the amount of rain depends on the region of Israel. The farther north and west you travel, the more rain will fall. Conversely, the farther south and east you travel, the drier it becomes. Since rain is sparse, Israel only sees

42

rainfall about 40–60 days per year. In the north, there are between 20 and 40 inches (50–100 cm) per year (60 in. or 152 cm on Mount Hermon). However, in the far southeast in Eilat, there is only an average rainfall of one-half inch (1.25 cm) per year, and no more than 1–2 inches (2.5–5 cm) per year along the Dead Sea and in Jericho!

43

It is a remarkable fact that Jerusalem and London share the same annual average rainfall of 22 inches (55 cm) per year! The difference is that in Jerusalem it all falls within about 50 days in heavy downpours, whereas in London, it is spread over some 300 days.[9]

With so few days of rain, how 44 do the trees, fields, and plants of Israel survive?

Dew is to be found in abundance in the coastal plains as well as the western side of the mountains, and the moisture-laden sea air rises each evening. Dew falls about 260 days per year, amounting to a remarkable 9–11 inches (23–28 cm) of water per year, which waters the plants during the summer months (April through November) when rain does not fall.

On most evenings in Israel, even in the summer, dew is dripping off of the rocks and parked cars onto the ground by 9 or 10 p.m., attesting to the wisdom of the farmers leaving small rocks in the soil among the crops to collect the dew that drips into the soil. The dew is a great 45 blessing of the Lord in a dry land.

One scholar suggested that the stark differences in the land of Israel between the wetter western and northern regions versus the drier eastern and southern regions could be equated with the biblical phrase, "the land of milk and honey." Dr. James Fleming suggests that the "land of milk" is the drier southern and eastern regions, where the herds of sheep, goats, and camel lived that provided milk and cheese — the Judean and Negev Deserts. This land is unpredictable, silent, lonely, and exhausting. Yet, it was here where God spoke most frequently to His people. Maybe it was because they were the most needy in these areas and needed God's help, so they called upon Him and He answered and provided.

On the other hand, the "land of honey" is the wetter western and northern regions where flowering trees could grow — the fertile coastal plains and Galilee. Yet these areas had more people and cities, and life was predictable, noisy, busy, and easy. Here, it was easy to miss God's voice and be so self-sufficient that God was not asked for anything.

While those on the dry "right stage" wondered if there would be a harvest and water for the coming year, those on the wetter "left stage" were reaping 50-fold, 75-fold, and 100-fold, with their cisterns full and springs flowing. While having plenty is a good thing to thank God for, if it distracts us from our daily reliance upon God, and getting more is the focus of our attention, then it becomes an idol.

Rain in Israel can be torrential. Visitors are usually surprised at the intensity of the rain in the winter that is most often accompanied by high winds. In Jerusalem, most of the winter rains seem to blow sideways and an umbrella is often of little use.

46

In the desert, the dry riverbeds, called *wadis* in Arabic and *nahalim* in Hebrew, can be flooded, as flash floods bring a wall of water down these valleys. It is dangerous to hike in the Judean Desert in the winter, because it need not be raining in the desert at all to be caught in one of these flash floods. That is because when it rains up on the ridge between Shechem and Hebron, the water that flows east to the Jordan Valley can catch hikers off guard in an unexpected flash flood.

It is an amazing sight to be driving along the Dead Sea and see huge waterfalls pouring off the 1,000 feet (305 m) cliffs that traverse the edge of the sea. It is so strong that it can wash out the road in a matter of minutes, and be over in a matter of hours.

The rain can be so localized that one *wadi* can become a torrent, while another *wadi* just a few miles away remains dry.

47   The ground in the desert is bone dry and does not absorb the rain, which accounts for the huge volume of water that makes up the flash floods. It has been estimated that only three percent of the rainfall in the desert regions actually penetrates the surface, while the rest either runs into the sea or quickly evaporates.[10]

A flash flood in a usually dry desert valley.

When the rain falls in Jerusalem, because 48
it is located on the watershed line, half of the
rainfall travels east through the Judean Desert
into the Dead Sea, while the other half goes
through the valleys to the west, taking the water
to coastal plain and to the Mediterranean Sea.

49

God always used rain, or the lack thereof,
to show His blessing or displeasure in the way
His people, Israel, were behaving.

In Deuteronomy we hear God saying,
"So, if you faithfully obey the commands I
am giving you today — to love the LORD your
God and to serve him with all your heart and
with all your soul — then I will send rain on
your land in its season, both autumn and spring rains, so
that you may gather in your grain, new wine and oil. I will
provide grass in the fields for your cattle, and you will eat
and be satisfied. Be careful or you will be enticed to turn
away and worship other gods and bow down to them. Then
the LORD's anger will burn against you, and he will shut the
heavens so that it will not rain and the ground will yield no
produce, and you will soon perish from the good land the
LORD is giving you" (Deut. 11:13–17).

In a similar vein, this theme is repeated in Deuteronomy
28, the well-known chapter on blessing and cursing for
Israel: "If you fully obey the LORD your God and carefully
follow all his commands that I give you today. . . . The LORD
will open the heavens, the storehouse of his bounty, to send
rain on your land in season and to bless all the work of your
hands" (Deut. 28:1–12).

On the other hand, God says, "However, if you do not
obey the LORD your God and do not carefully follow all his
commands and decrees I am giving you today. . . . The LORD
will turn the rain of your country into dust and powder;

it will come down from the skies until you are destroyed"
(Deut. 28:15–24).

All through history and even today, spe- **50**
cial prayers for rain are recited during the fall
festival of Sukkot, looking ahead to the rainy
season. It is considered a special blessing if there
is an "early rain" shower during the week-long
Sukkot (Feast of Tabernacles) festival. Also,
when the rain ceases to fall in Israel and drought
is looming on the horizon, it gives the people of
Israel pause to consider their actions and many turn out to
pray, asking God to forgive their sins and send the rain.

51 It is the rainy season which makes Israel a

paradise of flowers in the months of February
and March. For a few weeks the whole land
becomes a riot of color and scent, the air filled
with the singing of birds and the hum of in-
sects. This annual miracle of resurrection never
fails to capture the imagination of all who witness it. It is an unforgettable experience to see
hills red with anemones and poppies, fields blue with wild
blue lupines or pink or white cyclamen amongst the rocks,
the solitary beauty of an iris or the orchids that appear between the thistles.[11] This display is impressive because of the
abundance and variety of the flowers that bloom in such a
short span of time. The pilgrims who have only seen the dry
hills of the land of Israel in the summer or fall
are amazed when they get the chance to witness **52**
the flowering landscape in the spring.

The desert plants concentrate their whole life
cycle into one short season of a few months in
which they germinate, grow leaves, blossom, and

grow fruit to bear enough seeds for the next year. If there is a drought, these seeds can lie dormant for years, even centuries, waiting for the water to germinate and start the cycle all over again. Some trees and shrubs drop all of their leaves to conserve water and they look like dead sticks. Yet when water comes, they spring forth with life. It does not take much water to make the desert plants happy.

53   In the 1980s, we had one particularly wet winter that poured so much water on the desert that flowers were seen which had never been seen in the past. Out of the bleak, chalk hillsides of the Judean Desert emerged huge irises and other flowering plants that had waited for years for the right amount of water to show off their glory.

Annually, I am always amazed at the millions of red anemones that carpet the Judean Desert just east of Jerusalem in the spring after the winter rains. They bloom for just a few days and then disappear until the next year. God's creation is truly amazing.

Jesus used this image to teach us of the foolishness of worrying when He said, "And why do you worry about clothes? See how the lilies of the field grow. They do not labour or spin. Yet, I tell you that not even Solomon in all his splendour was dressed like one of these. If that is how God clothes the grass of the field, which is here today and tomorrow is thrown into the fire, will he not much more clothe you, O you of little faith?" (Matt. 6:28–30).

In most countries, there is a variety of terrain and climates. However, these variations are often widely separated and the transition between the zones is gradual. This is not the case in Israel, where we find five distinct geographical and climatic zones that change with such abruptness that in some places you can literally stand on the line where one zone shifts to another.

54

To illustrate just how close the changes are, I remember one ski trip I took to Mount Hermon where the snow was absolutely perfect powder. High up on the ski lift with cold alpine air blowing on the clear crisp day, I could look down 9,000 feet (2743 m) into the Jordan Valley and the Sea of Galilee where bananas were growing and holiday makers were water skiing. I could also see straight across the entire Galilee region of northern Israel and southern Lebanon, right to the shores of the Mediterranean Sea.

What a magnificently blessed land! It may be small, but God truly made it the "glory of all lands."

55

The five vegetation zones found in Israel include:

1. The Euro-Siberian zone, representing the kind of vegetation which is found in Europe, Russia, and Siberia.

2. The Mediterranean zone, in which we find conditions similar to those in countries bordering the Mediterranean Sea.

3. The Irano-Turanian zone, characterized by the same kind of steppe-land that exists in a wide area from Israel to China, stretching through Iran to the Gobi Desert of Inner Mongolia.

4. The Saharo-Arabian zone, which is pure desert and covers most of the Sahara in Africa, the Arabian peninsula, and parts of southern Iran.

5. The Sudanese zone of tropical vegetation, which in Israel is confined to some small but very interesting enclaves and oases.[12]

These five distinct zones and the geographical position of the land of Israel linking the three continents make Israel the meeting ground of plants and animals native to widely differing parts of the earth — plants with such differing origins as Siberia, Western Europe, Inner Asia, North Africa, and East Africa.

56

Considering the smallness of the land of Israel, it is amazing to realize that so much variety and diversity can be packed into this tiny land.

Think about where apples and oranges are grown, or strawberries and bananas. They grow in diverse places around the world. Certainly not in the same location, or even in the same region, as they are fruits that grow in either tropical or cold climates and are grown far apart from one another. However, all of them are grown in Israel, and it is not unusual to find warm and cold climate fruit trees in the same garden. Is this not part of God's declaration that Israel will be the "glory of all lands" (Ezek. 20:6; NASB)?

57

Most of us have read in the Bible about the "rose of Sharon" or the "lilies of the field" without realizing that no other land in the world has a wealth of plant life within so small an area as the land of Israel.

There are some 3,000 different species of plants in tiny Israel. This compares remarkably with 1,800 plant species in the British Isles, an area two and a half times the size of Israel, or with the 1,500 plant species in Egypt, an area ten times the size of

Israel and boasting one of the largest and most fertile areas in the Middle East, the Nile Delta![13]

For many of these plants, the land of Israel represents the extremity of their distribution. It is the eastern limit for many of the Mediterranean plants, the western limit of a number of Asian steppe-land plants, the northern most extremity of African plants, and the southernmost extremity of the Euro-Siberian plants. This is one of the unique features of the land of Israel.[14]

58

One example is the Doum palms, just north of Eilat, which are native to East Africa. There are only three clumps of these palms in Israel, their nearest relatives being found 1,000 miles to the south. No one knows how they came to Israel. In Ein Gedi, an ever-flowing freshwater spring on the cliffs overlooking the Dead Sea, you will find delicate maidenhair fern that would be scorched to oblivion by the hot, desert heat only a few yards away, or if the water stopped flowing.

59

Sometimes, one finds a ravine running east to west, where the southern wall, facing north and therefore cooler, is covered with Mediterranean plants, while the northern wall, facing south and therefore more dry and hot, supports only steppe-loving plants, and on the valley floor between them is an intermingling of both types of plant-life.[15]

In Israel, the Middle East custom among both Jews and Arabs is to plant fruit trees on the land around your house. I always find it amazing to find plants of typically different zones growing in the same garden; for example, the avocado and orange growing alongside an apple and a pear tree, with a grape arbor hanging over the patio!

In Israel there are seven species of produce that are considered by the Jewish people to represent the ancient blessing of God's fruitfulness to the land of Israel. They are dates, pomegranates, olives, figs, grapes, wheat, and barley. You see these symbols in Jewish art, on ancient coins and stone carvings for building decorations, embroidered or painted on Shabbat hallah bread covers, etc.

60

61

Because Israel is so mountainous, most of the farming in Israel is done on terraces. The native limestone erodes in stepped plates, making it very easy to build the terraces. You simply place stone walls in rows cascading down the slope about every 12–15 feet (3.5–4.5 m) and backfill it with soil until level. The custom is to plant fruit, olive, or almond trees on the terrace, with wheat or barley underneath.

In Matthew, we find the parable of the sower (Matt. 13:1–23). In this passage, the sower scatters his seed, which falls alternately on the path, on rocky places, among thorns, and on good soil. The birds ate what was on the path, that which sprouted on the rocky places withered and died, that which grew among the thorns was choked, and that which fell on good soil produced 100, 60, or 30 times what was sown.

62

Jesus equated the seed as the gospel, or the Word of God, being sown in the hearts of men. Only a portion of that gospel seed which is sown grows up to bear fruit. For others, it sprouts and quickly dies out, or is choked off early in its growth. When examining terrace farming in Israel, you quickly see how relevant this parable is to everyday life, and it tells us more about the meaning of the parable.

The farmer walks along a path on the upper edge of the terrace about three feet (1 m) from the wall of the terrace above. Because terraces are built on the slope of the mountains, the upper edge of the terrace has rocky outcroppings of bedrock. Then, in the shallow soil zone between the footpath and the rocky outcroppings, there is a narrow area where low thorn bushes grow naturally all over Israel. On the downside of the footpath is a large fertile growing area where the seed grows and produces. Just as the parable describes the sower, you can see it on any terrace in Israel. Interestingly, the largest zone of the terrace is the good soil, which should assure us that most of the seed of the gospel that we sow will grow and prosper.

63

The "good soil" of the parable of the sower (Matt. 13:8) looks quite rocky to farmers from non-arid lands. The rocks are left in the soil so that the crops can grow. Why, you may ask?

I already mentioned that 9–11 inches (22.5–28 cm) of dew fall upon Israel in the dry months of the year. The rocks, which cool quickly once the hot summer sun sets, will collect the heavy dew in the air as it condenses at night and then drips it onto the soil. The rocks also keep the moisture from evaporating so quickly the next morning when the hot sun rises.

Today, in Israel, you can still see terraces 64 that date back to the days of the Israelites and the time of King David. They have been perpetually maintained by those who have farmed the land since those ancient days. Around ancient biblical villages like Ein Kerem, the birthplace of John the Baptist, located near Jerusalem, the ancient terraces still have the seven species growing upon them: grapes, olives, almonds, dates, pomegranates, wheat, and barley.

65 Most people who don't live in a desert region consider the desert a dry and lifeless area. However, that is far from the case, especially in Israel. The deserts of Israel are teeming with plant and animal life, including ibex, turtles, snakes, and lizards, not to mention sheep, goats, camels, and even leopards.

In the Matthew 6 passage about worrying, 66 Jesus says, "Look at the birds of the air; they do not sow or reap or store away in barns, and yet your heavenly Father feeds them. Are you not much more valuable than they?" (Matt. 6:26).

The "birds of the air" have always been quite busy over the skies of Israel. The Bible speaks of the sparrow, eagle, raven, vulture, stork, and swallow. However, there are many more.

There are some 450 species of birds found in Israel, which is a huge number considering the size of this land. In the British Isles, there are 460 species, and even when you add Europe and Russia, a vastly larger area, there are 800 species.[16] The United States has 725 species of birds in an area 461 times bigger than Israel.

67  So what accounts for so many birds in Israel? The land of Israel provides highways linking three continents not only for man, but for the birds as well. Some birds migrate between the northern and southern hemispheres and cannot fly over the broad Mediterranean Sea. Therefore, flight patterns between lands as far south as South Africa to lands far in the north, including Greenland, the United Kingdom, Lapland, and northern Russia, all converge over Israel. For other birds, as with some plants, Israel is their southernmost destination or northernmost limit, depending on the continent on which they live.

Storks

One of the most exciting events of the year is when the huge flocks of storks traverse the skies over Jerusalem. I can stand on our porch and watch them for hours, as thousands of storks swirl in circular patterns on the air currents. They are such large birds; it is a fantastic spectacle.

The Great Rift Valley, including Israel's Arava and Jordan Valley, is their visual course of travel, and literally millions upon millions of different birds spend some time in Israel each year. It is truly a bird lover's paradise.

Remembering that the land of Israel is a con- 68
necting "hinge" between continents, it should be
no surprise to see the diversity of animals that
live or have lived in this land. There are represen-
tatives from all continents found in Israel.

At one time, the African lion, hippopota-
mus, warthog, hartebeest, rhinoceros, crocodile,
cheetah, and Syrian bear all lived in Israel.

Remember the Bible story where some youths mocked
Elisha who cursed them? "Then two bears came out of the
woods and mauled forty-two of the youths" (2 Kings 2:24).

We also can recount when David, as a youth, was a
shepherd and protected his flocks from lions and bears
(1 Sam. 17:33–37), one animal being from Africa and the
other from Europe, yet both found in Israel! David used
this information to convince Saul that he could overcome
Goliath, when he said, "Your servant has killed both the
lion and the bear; this uncircumcised Philistine will be like
one of them, because he has defied the armies of the living
God" (1 Sam. 17:36).

The last crocodile in the region was shot in 1917 by a
German soldier. Today, alligators have been re-introduced
to Israel. They are thriving in the hot springs of Hamat Ga-
der at the southern end of the Golan Heights near the Sea
of Galilee, and on game farms.

69   Today, we can still find in Israel such exotic
animals as leopards, lynxes, jungle cats, ibex,
gazelles, wild goats, hyenas, jackals, wolves,
foxes, wild boar, badgers, porcupines, and
polecats. The land of Israel is the southernmost
limit for the Siberian wolf, which illustrates just
how diverse and unique this land is.

The Bible often uses the characteristics of animals
found in the land of Israel to illustrate something about our

relationship to the Lord. Psalm 42:1–2, for example, says, "As the deer pants for streams of water, so my soul pants for you, O God. My soul thirsts for God, for the living God. When can I go and meet with God?"

Living here in the land of Israel, it never ceases to amaze me when I see the ibex antelope on the craggy cliffs of the Judean Desert. On one occasion, my family and I were rappelling down the cliffs overlooking the salty Dead Sea near the springs of Ein Gedi. Hang-ing from the dry, rocky cliffs

An ibex

1,000 feet (305 m) above the level of the sea, we saw an ibex enjoying the same view. In the blistering heat of the desert, it is easy to imagine this ibex longing for the sweet water of the springs of Ein Gedi. The rocky path to his destination was not easy, but the journey was worth it. We should be just as anxious to get into the presence of God.

70  The Gulf of Eilat, an extension of the Red Sea along the eastern shores of the Sinai peninsula, boasts one of the three richest cor-al reefs in the world. Not only is there coral, but also a symphony of fish and plant life that gives one a thrill when you don a snor-kel and mask and go take an "up close and personal" look for yourself. It is so exciting and beautiful, you simply want to share the news of what

you have seen with someone else. Because the desert has an extremely small amount of rainfall, there is no run-off and therefore no silt to cloud the waters. It is crystal clear. The area around Eilat with its huge granite mountains plunging into the azure sea makes it one of the world's resort destinations.

71

Since the Suez Canal opened more than a century ago, there has been a remarkable invasion of tropical marine organisms from the Red Sea into the Mediterranean — over 200 species in fact. Over 30 Red Sea species of fish alone have been counted, fish which have emigrated to the eastern Mediterranean and which have gained commercial importance for fishing along the coasts of Israel and Egypt. The providence is a further illustration of the way in which this region is the meeting place, not only of continents, but of seas as well! So real is this invasion, future specialists in this area will have to view the eastern Mediterranean as a distinct sub-region of the Mediterranean proper, characterized by an admixture of some 20 percent Indo-Pacific marine fauna.[17]

72

When the Lord described the land of Israel as "the glory of all lands" (Ezek. 20:6; NASB), the Hebrew word used for "glory" is not the usual term, but one which means "beauty" or "honor," as well as "glory." It is also the word used for "gazelle." This aptly describes the land of Israel, for the beauty and the glory of the gazelle are indeed unique. Israel is "the glory of all lands," and the more we explore it and seek to understand it, the more accurate we discover the Words of the Lord to be.[18]

CHAPTER THREE

COVENANTS AND THE LAND AND PEOPLE

73   The land of Canaan, later called Israel, was given by God to Abraham and his descendants as an everlasting possession. "The LORD appeared to Abram and said, 'To your offspring I will give this land' " (Gen. 12:7).

In Genesis 13:15, He repeated His promise when He said, "All the land that you see I will give to you and your offspring for ever." He said the same thing in Genesis 15:18, "To your descendants I give this land."

The land of Canaan that Abraham saw was a land of mountains and fertile valleys.

God "cut a covenant" with Abram to confirm His promises to Abram, including that this
land belonged to him and his descendants forever. "He [God] also said to him [Abram], 'I am
the LORD, who brought you out of Ur of the
Chaldeans to give you this land to take possession of it.' But Abram said, 'O Sovereign LORD,
how can I know that I shall gain possession of
it?' So the LORD said to him, 'Bring me a heifer, a goat and a
ram, each three years old, along with a dove and a young pi-
geon.' Abram brought all these to him, cut them in two and
arranged the halves opposite each other; the birds, however,
he did not cut in half. Then birds of prey came down on the
carcasses, but Abram drove them away" (Gen. 15:7–11).

74

In Bible days, a covenant promise was confirmed by the
spilling of blood and a sacrifice. The birds of prey, representing those who oppose the plans of God, tried to steal
the elements of this covenant.

75

After Abram cut the covenant, he fell into a
deep sleep and God told him two things concerning the land.

First, that his descendants would be slaves
in a country that was not theirs for 400 years,
but they would come out with great possessions
and come into the Promised Land (Gen. 15:12–
16). This happened in the land of Egypt, after
the time of Jacob. Four hundred years later, Moses led them
out in the great Exodus back to the Promised Land.

Second, a smoking firepot and blazing torch passed
between the halves of the sacrifice. It was God walking between them, accepting the offering (Gen. 15:17) and He said
to Abram: "To your descendants, I give this land, from the
river of Egypt to the great river, the Euphrates — the land
of the Kenites, Kenizzites, Kadmonites, Hittites, Perizzites,

Raphaites, Amorites, Canaanites, Girgashites and Jebusites" (Gen. 15:18–21).

When Abram was 99 years old, he still had 76 no son with Sarah, his wife. It seems he must have been feeling in his heart that the promise was not to be. However, we see in Genesis 17 how God came to him to reconfirm the promise of a son, descendants, and a land. Abram was greatly blessed by this, fell on his face before the Lord, and God changed his name to Abraham to confirm this renewed promise.

"Abram fell facedown, and God said to him, 'As for me, this is my covenant with you: You will be the father of many nations. No longer will you be called Abram; your name will be Abraham, for I have made you a father of many nations. I will make you very fruitful; I will make nations of you, and kings will come from you. I will establish my covenant as an everlasting covenant between me and you" (Gen. 17:3–7).

77 In this same passage, God again confirmed His promise about the land being for Abraham and his descendants, and it was an unconditional covenant from God himself. "I will establish my covenant as an everlasting covenant between me and you and your descendants after you for the generations to come, to be your God and the God of your descendants after you. The whole land of Canaan, where you are now an alien, I will give as an everlasting possession to you and your descendants after you; and I will be their God" (Gen. 17:7–8). Three times in two verses, God emphasized that it was an everlasting covenant to Abraham and his descendents. Therefore, it still exists today!

Immediately after confirming this covenant, God gave Abraham and his descendants the covenant mark of circumcision to show this covenant between God, His land, and Abraham's offspring. The descendants of Abraham, Isaac, and Jacob became known as God's chosen people.

78

It was God who introduced the covenant mark of circumcision. "Then God said to Abraham, 'As for you, you must keep my covenant, you and your descendants after you for the generations to come. This is my covenant with you and your descendants after you, the covenant you are to keep: Every male among you shall be circumcised. You are to undergo circumcision, and it will be the sign of the covenant between me and you. For the generations to come every male among you who is eight days old must be circumcised. . . . My covenant in your flesh is to be an everlasting covenant" (Gen. 17:9–13).

79

Since that day and unto this day, all Jewish male children undergo what is called a *Brit Mila*, the "covenant of circumcision." It is performed on the eighth day after birth, to mark them as a descendant of Abraham, Isaac, and Jacob. This religious ceremony is faithfully observed by all Jews, so that they will remember they are part of, and responsible to maintain, God's promise to Abraham.

80

At this time, Abraham already had a son (whose name was Ishmael) by Hagar. Ishmael was 13 years old (the age of accountability), and Abraham inquired of God if Ishmael was the one to receive the blessings of the covenant and the land. However, the answer was "No,"

*Ishmael and Isaac
were destined to
inherit separate
kingdoms.*

as God's land was
not given to the
descendants of
Ishmael (one ances-
tor of many Middle
Eastern peoples), but
rather to Isaac and his
descendents, the Jewish people.

In Genesis 17:18, "Abraham said to God, 'If only Ishmael might live under your blessing!' " But God's answer
was, and is, very clear — that the covenant would not be
with Ishmael, but with Isaac.

In Genesis 17:19, God said to Abraham, "Your wife
Sarah will bear you a son, and you will call him Isaac. I will
establish my covenant with him as an everlasting covenant
for his descendants after him." Then, for emphasis, God said
again, "But my covenant I will establish with Isaac, whom
Sarah will bear to you by this time next year" (Gen. 17:21).

God promised to bless Ishmael and to make   81
him a great nation: "And as for Ishmael, I have
heard you: I will surely bless him; I will make
him fruitful and will greatly increase his numbers. He will be the father of twelve rulers, and I
will make him into a great nation" (Gen. 17:20).

However, the bloodline of the covenant
promise concerning the land would go through
Isaac, not Ishmael: "In Isaac your descendants shall be
called" (Heb. 11:18; NASB).

82  This land was not given to the other sons of Abraham, but only to Isaac.

After Sarah died, Abraham had six more sons by Ketura, as well as others by his concubines, who are ancestors of many of the Middle Eastern peoples today. However, the covenant of the land was not for them: "Now Abraham gave all he had to Isaac; but to the sons of his concubines, Abraham gave gifts while he was still living, and sent them away from his son Isaac eastward, to the land of the east" (Gen. 25:5–6; NASB). Note that Abraham also blessed these sons, but sent them away from the land of Canaan.

God spoke directly to Isaac to confirm to 83 him the promises He made with Isaac's father Abraham: "Stay in this land for a while, and I will be with you and will bless you. For to you and your descendants I will give all these lands and will confirm the oath I swore to your father Abraham" (Gen. 26:3).

84  This land and covenant were given only to Isaac's son Jacob and his descendants, not Esau and his descendants. Jacob received the birthright from his father, Isaac, when Isaac blessed Jacob and said: "May he [God] give you and your descendants the blessing given to Abraham, so that you may take possession of the land where you now live as an alien, the land God gave to Abraham" (Gen. 28:4). 85

God also spoke directly to Jacob: "I am the LORD, the God of your father Abraham and the God of Isaac. I will give you and your descendants the land on which you are lying.

Your descendants will be like the dust of the earth, and you will spread out to the west and to the east, to the north and to the south. All peoples on earth will be blessed through you and your offspring. I am with you and will watch over you wherever you go, and I will bring you back to this land. I will not leave you until I have done what I have promised you" (Gen. 28:13–15).

86   God changed Jacob's name to Israel, meaning, "he struggles with God," after he wrestled with God at Peniel: " 'Your name will no longer be Jacob, but Israel, because you have struggled with God and with men and have overcome' " (Gen. 32:28).

Because God changed Jacob's name, his descendants through Jacob's 12 sons were known as the tribes of Israel, the Children of Israel, and Israelites (Gen. 32:32; Exod. 1:12; 9:7; John 1:47; Rom. 9:4; 11:1). The land of Canaan became known as the land of Israel, which has passed on unto this day. One of the names of God is the God of Israel (Gen. 33:20; Exod. 34:23).

In the Bible, God's covenant people, the descendants of Abraham, Isaac, and Jacob, were called by many other descriptive and poetic names: the Hebrews (Exod. 10:3; 1 Sam. 4:6), the house of Israel (Exod. 40:38; Josh. 21:45), a holy people (Deut. 7:6; 14:2, 21), my people (Exod. 3:7; Exod. 10:3), my son, my firstborn (Exod. 4:22–23), treasured possession (Exod. 19:5; Deut. 26:18), a people of inheritance (Deut. 4:20), my ancient people (Isa. 44:7).[1]

87

88 What happened to Esau? According to Genesis 36:6–8, Esau took his descendants and all his possessions and went to another land away from his brother Jacob. Esau lived in the hill country of Seir, which is east of the Dead Sea on the east side of the Jordan Valley. The Bible tells us that Esau is Edom (Gen. 36:1).

It specifically tells us that the descendants of Esau are the Edomites, and Israel was not their land.

The Book of Obadiah is a proclamation of doom upon the sons of Esau (Edom) for their constant persecution of the descendants of Jacob (Israel): "Because of the violence against your brother Jacob, you will be covered with shame; you will be destroyed for ever" (Obad. 1:10).

I have no bitterness toward the descendants 89 of Ishmael, Esau, or the other sons of Abraham, nor do I wish to be unkind to our Arab and Middle Eastern friends, some of whom claim Abrahamic rights as descendants of these sons. However, I must be faithful to what the Bible teaches concerning God's land. He gave it as an everlasting covenant to the descendants of Abraham, Isaac, and Jacob, only. God chose them to work out His redemptive plan that would bless the world out of this land. Isaiah says, "The law will go out from Zion, the word of the LORD from Jerusalem" (Isa. 2:3). The covenant and plan is still in force today.

90 The land of Israel, given to Abraham and his descendants, was as important to God's redemptive plan as were the people.

In Genesis 12:1–3, we read, "The LORD had said to Abram, 'Leave your country, your people and your father's household and go to the land I will show you. I will make you into a great nation and I will bless you; I will make your name great, and you will be a blessing. I will bless those who bless you, and whoever curses you I will curse; and all the peoples on earth will be blessed through you."

Israel was, and is, located in the center of the ancient world, and all transportation and communication between the continents had to pass through this territory to reach the other. In doing so, the travelers, merchants, traders, and even the armies encountered the Children of Israel and saw the works and testimony of the Lord in their midst.

91

They were a chosen people for three purposes: to worship God in this land and show the world the blessing of serving the one true God of the universe; to receive, record, and transmit the Word of God (through them we have our Bible); and finally, to be the human channel for the Messiah from whom we have our salvation.

God told His people, "And now, O Israel, what does the LORD your God ask of you but to fear [awe] the LORD your God, to walk in all his ways, to love him, to serve the LORD your God with all your heart and with all your soul, and to observe the LORD's commands and decrees that I am giving you today for your own good?" (Deut. 10:12–13).

Truly, the whole world has been blessed with the salvation of God through Jesus, our Savior, who came to us as a descendant of Abraham, Isaac, and Jacob, the root of Jesse, of the line of David, because of the faithfulness of God and His people, Israel.

92

In order for God to protect His purposes for the Children of Israel in the land of Israel, He promised to bless those who blessed

Abraham and his descendants and curse those who cursed them. This blessing and cursing we have seen throughout the history of Israel, not only in relation to the land of Israel, but also in relation to the Children of Israel, the Jewish people. Those peoples and nations which blessed the land and people of Israel have been blessed, and those who have come against them have been cursed. One can hopscotch through history to find examples of God's blessings and curses to the nations who blessed or cursed Israel.

God always cursed those who sought to destroy His people. The kings of the Jordan Valley who rose up against Abram were utterly destroyed and their wealth given over to Abram (Gen. 14). When Pharaoh blessed Joseph, his land was blessed (Gen. 41). However, when a pharaoh rose up who "knew Joseph no more" and enslaved the Hebrews, then Egypt was cursed (Exod. 9–12). When Sennacherib, king of Assyria, tried to conquer Jerusalem and defeat good King Hezekiah, God killed his army on the hills around Jerusalem (2 Chron. 32). When Haman plotted to destroy all the Jews of Media-Persia, God foiled his plot and he was killed on the gallows he built to kill the Jews (Esther).

There were many more nations defeated or humbled from their lofty heights of power and prestige, some to total ruin, because they came against Israel and the Jews. The list goes on with the major players being the Babylonians, Greeks, Romans, Muslims, the crusaders, Spanish inquisitors, the Russians who perpetrated the Pogroms, and the Nazis who perpetrated the Holocaust. In our day, Saddam Hussein rained down Scud missiles upon Israel and was ultimately defeated and ousted from his despotic rule.

94 God always blessed those peoples and nations who blessed Israel. Here are a few of many examples: When Solomon built the first temple to the Lord, Hiram, king of Tyre who helped Solomon with timber from the cedars of Lebanon, was blessed by this alliance (2 Chron. 2). The queen of Sheba's blessings to Solomon resulted in great blessing on her land of Sheba (Ethiopia) (2 Chron. 9). Turkey, who took in the Jews when they were expelled from Spain and Portugal in the 15th century, was blessed by these newcomers and became a great power, conquering the entire Middle East shortly thereafter. In our day, the United States of America, who has protected its Jewish citizens and been the best friend Israel has had in the world, is also a blessed nation.

God promised to judge His people if they disobeyed Him. That is true for each of us. However, Scripture does not say that Israel's disobedience would cause them to forfeit their gift and covenant of the land and their national status as His people. Deuteronomy 28 shows that God's pronouncement of blessing and cursing only affected the quality of life of the Israelites, which was conditional upon their faithfulness to Him. The promise of the land was not based upon Israel's performance, but upon God's oath and character. He gave this land to Abraham and his descendants as an everlasting possession. He cannot lie, nor does He make promises He does not fulfill (Num. 23:19).   95

96  In Deuteronomy 30:1–10, even before the Children of Israel entered into the Promised Land, God knew they would violate His statutes and be exiled from the land at a time in the

future. Yet, He also declared that He would gather them back into the land He had given their forefathers and prosper them, as they would obey and trust in Him. "When all these blessings and curses I have set before you come upon you and you take them to heart wherever the LORD your God disperses you among the nations, and when you and your children return to the LORD your God and obey him with all your heart and with all your soul according to everything I command you today, then the LORD your God will restore your fortunes and have compassion on you and gather you again from all the nations where he scattered you. Even if you have been banished to the most distant land under the heavens, from there the LORD your God will gather you and bring you back. He will bring you to the land that belonged to your fathers, and you will take possession of it. He will make you more prosperous and numerous than your fathers" (Deut. 30:1–5).

God's covenant with the Jewish people concerning the land of Israel, which He gave to them, is forever and unbreakable. In Psalm 89:30–37, we read, "If his sons forsake my law and do not follow my statues, if they violate my decrees and fail to keep my commands, I will punish their sin with the rod, their iniquity with flogging; but I will not take my love from him, nor will I ever betray my faithfulness. I will not violate my covenant or alter what my lips have uttered. Once for all, I have sworn by my holiness — and I will not lie to David — that his line will continue for ever and his throne endure before me like the sun; it will be established for ever like the moon, the faithful witness in the sky."

Here again, we see that sin would bring judgment and reprimand and affect their quality of life, but their actions would not break God's everlasting covenant between the Jewish people and the land.

98

Jeremiah gives physical proof of the surety of this covenant between the people and the land, when he declares, "This is what the Lord says, he who appoints the sun to shine by day, who decrees the moon and stars to shine by night, who stirs up the sea so that its waves roar — the Lord Almighty is his name: 'Only if these ordinances vanish from my sight,' declares the Lord, 'will the descendants of Israel ever cease to be a nation before me'" (Jer. 31:35–36).

The last time I checked, the sun was still shining in the sky by day, and the stars and the moon were still gracing the night sky. Therefore, because I believe that God's Word is true, I also believe He did not break His covenant with His people, Israel.

99

Israel's sin and subsequent exile from the land did not change their divine right to this land given to them by the Lord in covenant.

Many people have wrongly said that God's promise to give the Children of Israel this land was based upon Israel's faithfulness to God's laws, and that when they were disobedient and sent into captivity, this nullified God's promise. However, the Bible teaches otherwise.

In Leviticus 26:21–39, we read that God would punish Israel for her disobedience and send them into captivity. But, according to verses 44–45, God will bring them back: "Yet in spite of this, when they are in the land of their enemies, I will not reject them or abhor them so as to destroy them completely, breaking my covenant with them. I am the Lord their God. But for their sake I will remember the covenant with their ancestors whom I brought out of Egypt in the sight of the nations to be their God. I am the Lord."

"For the LORD will not reject his people; he will never forsake his inheritance" (Ps. 94:14).

"But you, O Israel, my servant, Jacob, whom I have chosen, you descendants of Abraham my friend, I took you from the ends of the earth, from its farthest corners I called you. I said, 'You are my servant'; I have chosen you and have not rejected you' " (Isa. 41:8–9).

100   Along with the promise of blessing, God promised the people of Israel that they would be destroyed if they did not follow the Lord: "If you ever forget the LORD your God and follow other gods and worship and bow down to them, I testify against you today that you will surely be destroyed. Like the nations the LORD destroyed before you, so you will be destroyed for not obeying the LORD your God" (Deut. 8:19–20).

The Jewish people, the descendants of Abraham, Isaac, and Jacob, are still alive as a people and again live in their ancient biblical land. This is more physical proof that God did not break His everlasting covenant between them and the land, or take His blessing away from them.

Four hundred years after these covenant promises were made to Abraham, Isaac, and Jacob, God confirmed His promises to the Children of Israel through Moses: "I am the LORD. I appeared to Abraham, to Isaac and to Jacob as God Almighty, but by my name the LORD I did not make myself known to them. I also established my covenant with them to give them the land of Canaan, where they lived as aliens" (Exod. 6:2–4).

101

God then goes on to tell Moses that He remembers His covenants and promises and that He would free them from slavery and take them out of Egypt, "And I will bring you to the land I swore with uplifted hand to give to Abraham, to Isaac and to Jacob. I will give it to you as a possession. I am the Lord" (Exod. 6:8).

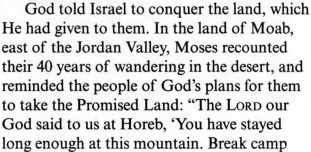

102 God told Israel to conquer the land, which He had given to them. In the land of Moab, east of the Jordan Valley, Moses recounted their 40 years of wandering in the desert, and reminded the people of God's plans for them to take the Promised Land: "The Lord our God said to us at Horeb, 'You have stayed long enough at this mountain. Break camp and advance into the hill country of the Amorites; go to all the neighboring peoples in the Arabah, in the mountains, in the western foothills, in the Negev and along the coast, to the land of the Canaanites and to Lebanon, as far as the great river, the Euphrates. See, I have given you this land. Go in and take possession of the land that the Lord swore he would give to your fathers — to Abraham, Isaac and Jacob — and to their descendants after them' " (Deut. 1:6–8).

God told the Israelites that they would not have to go into battle alone, but that He would fight for them to conquer the Promised Land: "I will be an enemy to your enemies and will oppose those who oppose you. My angel will go ahead of you and bring you into the land of the Amorites, Hittites, Perizzites, Canaanites, Hivites and Jebusites, and I will wipe them out" (Exod. 23:22–23). In reality, the Middle East conflict over the land of Israel was started by God.

103

104

God alone was to be worshiped in the land, not the idols of the pagans they would conquer, so that the Children of Israel would be blessed in the land:

"Do not bow down before their gods or worship them or follow their practices. You must demolish them and break their sacred stones to pieces. Worship the LORD your God, and his blessing will be on your food and water. I will take away sickness from among you, and none will miscarry or be barren in your land. I will give you a full life span" (Exod. 23:24–26).

"This is what you are to do to them: Break down their altars, smash their sacred stones, cut down their Asherah poles and burn their idols in the fire" (Deut. 7:5).

The pagan god Baal

God wanted all the pagans driven out of the Land so that they would not influence the Israelites to sin against God:

105

"I will establish your borders from the Red Sea to the Sea of the Philistines [Mediterranean], and from the desert [Sinai] to the [Euphrates] River. I will hand over to you the people who live in the land and you will drive them out before you. Do not make a covenant with them or with their gods. Do not let them live in your land, or they will cause you to sin against me, because the worship of their gods will certainly be a snare to you" (Exod. 23:31–33).

"When the Lord your God brings you into the land you are entering to possess and drives out before you many nations — the Hittites, Girgashites, Amorites, Canaanites, Perizzites, Hivites and Jebusites, seven nations larger and stronger than you — and when the Lord your God has delivered them over to you and you have defeated them, then you must destroy them totally. Make no treaty with them and show them no mercy. Do not intermarry with them. Do not give your daughters to their sons or take their daughters for your sons, for they will turn your sons away from following me to serve other gods, and the Lord's anger will burn against you and will quickly destroy you" (Deut. 7:1–4).

106   Unfortunately, the Israelites did not drive out all of the pagan tribes and they did succumb to worshiping their gods.

Three hundred and fifty cities mentioned in the Bible, where most of the Israelites lived, are in the drier eastern and southern "right stage" regions of Israel, where life was unpredictable, silent, lonely, and exhausting. Here is where God had their attention. However, in excavating Israelite houses in the mountains of Samaria, archaeologists found carved idols of their pagan neighbors who lived in the wetter, western, coastal plains, hidden under the floor stones. Perhaps the Israelites saw the abundance of these pagan tribes and thought to give their gods, Baal and Astarte, some attention. However, God was angered when His people chose the ways of the world over trusting Him.

Those Israelites who did this may have hidden their sin under the floor stones, but the truth of their deceptive actions has been revealed 3,000 years later. Truly, "your sin will find you out" (Num. 32:23).

God was also driving out the pagan tribes from His land because of their wickedness: "It is on account of the wickedness of these nations that the LORD is going to drive them out before you. . . . to accomplish what He swore to your fathers, to Abraham, Isaac and Jacob" (Deut. 9:4–5).

107

108

It was not God's plan, but man's disobedience, that caused the Children of Israel to wander in the desert for 40 years before going into the Promised Land. Shortly after leaving Egypt, one member from each tribe of Israel went to see the Promised Land. They reported to the people of the bounty of the land and they also described the strength of those living in the land: "But the people who live there are powerful, and the cities are fortified and very large. We even saw descendants of Anak there. The Amalekites live in the Negev; the Hittites, Jebusites and Amorites live in the hill country; and the Canaanites live near the sea and along the Jordan" (Num. 13:28–29).

The people became fearful and rebelled against God's plan to take the land. However, Joshua and Caleb stood on the Lord's side, saying, "The land we passed through and explored is exceedingly good. If the LORD is pleased with us, he will lead us into that land, a land flowing with milk and honey, and will give it to us. Only do not rebel against the LORD. And do not be afraid of the people of the land, because we will swallow them up. Their protection is gone, but the LORD is with us. Do not be afraid of them" (Num. 14:7–9).

Joshua and Caleb did not persuade the people, and God was angry with them for their lack of faith. It was at this point that God banished them to wandering in the desert for 40 years, and only Joshua and Caleb were promised that they would enter the Promised Land.

When it was time for Joshua to bring the next generation of the Children of Israel into the land, God repeated this command to conquer the Promised Land to Joshua: "Moses my servant is dead. 109

Now then, you and all these people, get ready to cross the Jordan River into the land I am about to give to them — to the Israelites. I will give you every place where you set your foot, as I promised Moses. Your territory will extend from the desert to Lebanon, and from the great river, the Euphrates — all the Hittite country — to the Great Sea on the west. No one will be able to stand up against you all the days of your life. As I was with Moses, so I will be with you; I will never leave you nor forsake you. Be strong and courageous, because you will lead these people to inherit the land I swore to their forefathers to give them" (Josh.1:2–6).

110

Joshua called his people to fulfill the promise of God and follow him in conquering the Promised Land. He told his people: "This is how you will know that the living God is among you and that he will certainly drive out before you the Canaanites, Hittites, Hivites, Perizzites, Girgashites, Amorites and Jebusites" (Josh. 3:10). He then told them how the Lord would part the floodwaters of the Jordan River so they could cross over to the other side. This is what happened and then the people knew that God was with them, and they conquered the land, region by region, starting with Jericho.

111

Joshua ordered his officers to prepare, saying, " 'Get your supplies ready. Three days from now, you will cross the Jordan here to go in and take possession of the land the LORD your God is giving you' " (Josh. 1:11).

On the day of the crossing of the Jordan, God gave them a sign that He was with them in battle. Joshua explained to the people, "This is how you will know that the living God is among you, and that he will certainly drive out before you the Canaanites, Hittites, Hivites, Perizzites, Girgashites, Amorites and Jebusites. See, the ark of the covenant of the Lord of all the earth will go into the Jordan ahead of you. Now then, choose twelve men from the tribes of Israel, one from each tribe. And as soon as the priests who carry the ark of the LORD — the Lord of all the earth — set foot in the Jordan, its waters flowing downstream will be cut off and stand up in a heap" (Josh. 3:10–13).

This is exactly what happened: "For the LORD your God dried up the Jordan before you until you had crossed over. The LORD your God did to the Jordan just what he had done to the Red Sea when he dried it up before us until we had crossed over. He did this so that all the peoples of the earth might know that the hand of the LORD is powerful and so that you might always fear the LORD your God" (Josh. 4:23–24).

112 God directed Joshua to drive all of the pagans out of the land and spare none. The Gibeonites, who lived in the mountains north and west of Jerusalem, deceived Joshua into making a covenant with them, saying they were from a distant land. Instead of praying to consult the Lord (Josh. 9:14), he acted in his flesh and made a grave error. Once discovered, he asked the Gibeonites why they deceived him.

The Gibeonites had heard about what Joshua and his army were doing and said to Joshua: "Your servants were clearly told how the LORD your God had commanded his servant Moses to give you the whole land and to wipe out all its inhabitants from before you. So we feared for our lives because of you, and that is why we did this. We are now in your hands. Do to us whatever seems good and right to you" (Josh. 9:24–25).

Joshua honored the treaty, but made the Gibeonites into woodcutters and water carriers, as servants to Israel. However, this area was not inhabited by Israel, and it later became a dividing line between the northern and southern kingdoms after Solomon.

Just as God had warned, those who were not expelled from the land would be a problem to Israel in the future.

Joshua systematically conquered the land **113** of Israel, and it was done in fulfillment of the promises of God to Abraham, Isaac, and Jacob: "So the LORD gave Israel all the land he had sworn to give their forefathers, and they took possession of it and settled there. The LORD gave them rest on every side, just as he had sworn to their forefathers. Not one of their enemies withstood them; the LORD handed all their enemies over to them. Not one of all the LORD's good promises to the house of Israel failed; every one was fulfilled" (Josh. 21:43–45).

114 The reality of conflict over the land of Israel is nothing new and it in no way indicates that God is not with the Jewish people concerning the land issue, even today.

I have heard Christians say that Israel today could not be part of God's plan, because there is so much war and strife that it can't be of God. However, since when has it been any different? All through the Old Testament, nations rose up to fight against the Jewish people, the descendants of Abraham, in the land of Israel. From the moment Joshua brought the Children of Israel into the Promised Land, it was a fight to possess the land. King David was seemingly at constant war with his neighbors, the Philistines. Why should it be surprising that conflict is still happening today? The enemies of God have always fought against His plans.

One of the first things that Joshua did after entering the Promised Land was to call the people together to Mount Ebal to renew the covenant between God, the people of Israel, and the land (Josh. 8:30–35). There, he had built an altar to the Lord and offered burnt offerings. Then "Joshua read all the words of the law — the blessings and the curses — just as it is written in the Book of the Law. There was not a word of all that Moses had commanded that Joshua did not read to the whole assembly of Israel, including the women and children, and the aliens who lived among them" (Josh. 8:34–35).

115

Mount Ebal

116

God called His people, Israel, to be a holy people and to live in His land to be a light to the nations, showing the blessedness of serving the one true God: "For you are a people holy to the LORD your God. The LORD your God has chosen you out of all the peoples on the face of the earth to be his people, his treasured possession" (Deut. 7:6).

God loved the people He chose to honor.   117
His covenant promises: "The LORD did not set
his affection on you and choose you because
you were more numerous than other peoples,
for you were the fewest of all peoples. But
it was because the LORD loved you and kept
the oath he swore to your forefathers that
he brought you out with a mighty hand and
redeemed you from the land of slavery, from the power of
Pharaoh king of Egypt. Know therefore that the LORD your
God is God; he is the faithful God, keeping his covenant of
love to a thousand generations of those who love him and
keep his commands" (Deut. 7:7–9).

118

King David proclaims the promise of God and the Israelites to the land of Canaan: "He is the LORD our God; his judgments are in all the earth. He remembers his covenant for ever, the word he commanded, for a thousand genera-tions, the covenant he made with Abraham, the oath he swore to Isaac. He confirmed it to Jacob as a decree, to Israel as an everlasting
covenant: 'To you I will give the land of Canaan as the por-tion you will inherit' " (1 Chron. 16:14–18).

King David also proclaims how God ful- **119**
filled His promise to Abraham for protection
of His descendants: "When they were but few
in number, few indeed, and strangers in it, they
wandered from nation to nation, from one
kingdom to another. He allowed no man to oppress them; for their sake he rebuked kings: 'Do
not touch my anointed ones; do my prophets
no harm' " (1 Chron. 16:19–22).

120

In the days of Ezra and Nehemiah, when
the Israelites returned from exile to rebuild
Jerusalem, they humbled themselves before the
Lord. Ezra read the whole law, just as Joshua
had done and the people confessed their sin
before the Lord. In proclaiming all that God
had done for them, they said: "You gave them
[their ancestors] kingdoms and nations, allot-
ting to them even the remotest frontiers. . . . You made their
sons as numerous as the stars in the sky, and you brought
them into the land that you told their fathers to enter and
possess. Their sons went in and took possession of the
land. You subdued before them the Canaanites, who lived
in the land; you handed the Canaanites over to them, along
with their kings and the peoples of the land, to deal with
them as they pleased. They captured fortified cities and
fertile land; they took possession of houses filled with all
kinds of good things, wells already dug, vineyards, olive
groves and fruit trees in abundance. They ate to the full and
were well-nourished; they revelled in your great **121**
goodness" (Neh. 9:22–25).

God has given the Children of Israel a position above all the peoples and nations of the
world:

"He has declared that he will set you in praise, fame and honour high above all the nations he has made and that you will be a people holy to the LORD your God, as he promised" (Deut. 26:19).

"The LORD will make you the head, not the tail. If you pay attention to the commands of the LORD your God that I give you this day and carefully follow them, you will always be at the top, never at the bottom" (Deut. 28:13).

122   God chose His people and His land, Israel, and considered them a treasured possession, which He loves:

"For the LORD has chosen Jacob to be his own, Israel to be his treasured possession" (Ps. 135:4).

"He has raised up for his people a horn, the praise of all his saints, of Israel, the people close to his heart. Praise the LORD" (Ps. 148:14).

"The LORD takes delight in his people; he crowns the humble with salvation" (Ps. 149:4).

For 4,000 years, God has had a covenant with His people, Israel, and desires His best for them.

The Children of Israel are a people who are 123
as a flock unto the Lord, whom He leads:

"But he brought his people out like a flock;
he led them like sheep through the desert"
(Ps. 78:52).

"The LORD their God will save them on
that day as the flock of his people. They will
sparkle in his land like jewels in a crown"
(Zech. 9:16).

124

The Children of Israel were protected by
God in Egypt and not affected by the plagues
that befell the Egyptians. These plagues were
spoken forth by Moses on Egypt because of the
stubbornness of Pharaoh who refused to let the
Children of Israel go.

Moses was told to go to Pharaoh and
tell him if he did not let the Hebrews go that
swarms of flies would infest Egypt.

" 'But on that day I will deal differently with the land
of Goshen, where my people live; no swarms of flies will
be there, so that you will know that I, the LORD am in this
land. I will make a distinction between my people and your
people. This miraculous sign will occur tomorrow' " (Exod.
8:22–23).

"And the next day, the LORD did it: All the livestock of
the Egyptians died, but not one animal belonging to the
Israelites died" (Exod. 9:6).

"The only place it did not hail was the land of Goshen,
where the Israelites were" (Exod. 9:26).

These events of divine protection from the plagues
continued occurring through the passing over of the Angel
of Death, sparing the houses of Israelites who applied the
blood on the doorpost of their homes.

God promised His people, Israel, the blessing of divine health: "I will take away sickness from among you, and none will miscarry or be barren in your land. I will give you a full life span" (Exod. 23:25–26).

125

126

God promised divine protection to His people, Israel:

" 'For whoever touches you touches the apple of his [God's] eye' " (Zech. 2:8).

"As the mountains surround Jerusalem, so the LORD surrounds his people both now and for evermore" (Ps. 125:2).

" 'And I myself will be a wall of fire around it,' declares the LORD, 'and I will be its glory within' " (Zech. 2:5).

"I will be an enemy to your enemies and will oppose those who oppose you" (Exod. 23:22).

God's people were promised prosperity:

"The LORD will send a blessing on your barns and on everything you put your hand to. The LORD your God will bless you in the land he is giving you" (Deut. 28:8).

"Then the LORD your God will make you most prosperous in all the work of your hands and in the fruit of your womb, the young of your livestock and the crops of your land" (Deut. 30:9).

127

128

The Children of Israel were promised strength and peace:

"The LORD gives strength to his people; the LORD blesses his people with peace" (Ps. 29:11).

"I will grant peace in the land, and you will lie down and no one will make you afraid.

I will remove savage beasts from the land, and the sword will not pass through your country. You will pursue your enemies, and they will fall by the sword before you. Five of you will chase a hundred, and a hundred of you will chase ten thousand, and your enemies will fall by the sword before you" (Lev. 26:6–8).

"So do not fear, for I am with you; do not be dismayed, for I am your God. I will strengthen you and help you; I will uphold you with my righteous right hand" (Isa. 41:10).

The covenant promises to Israel were also 129 extended to the Church, by the grace of God. In Ephesians 2:11–13, Paul tells the Gentile world that through the blood of Christ (the Messiah) we not only received our salvation, but became part of the covenant promises of God to Israel, and are even made citizens.

"Remember that at that time you were separate from Christ, excluded from citizenship in Israel and foreigners to the covenants of the promise, without hope and without God in the world. But now in Christ Jesus you who once were far away have been brought near through the blood of Christ" (Eph. 2:12–13).

Our gift of salvation through the blood of Christ is also a part of God's ongoing plan and blessing He made in covenant with Israel.

130 Paul makes it clear in his Epistle to the Galatians that in Christ we are also adopted sons of Abraham, and therefore are privy to the promise made to the seed of Abraham: "If you belong to Christ, then you are Abraham's seed, and heirs according to the promise" (Gal. 3:29). Note, however, as spiritual heirs, we become joint heirs along with Abraham's natural seed.

In Christ, we don't take over the promises. Rather, we are joined into them.

In a very clear and powerful word picture in Romans 11, Paul shows us the virtue and blessing of being grafted into the olive tree, a symbol which represents the promises and covenants of God that are eternal.

131

In this passage, we Gentiles (the Church) are referred to as the "wild olive branches" grafted into the olive tree among the "natural olive branches," which are the Jewish people, the natural descendants of Abraham, Isaac, and Jacob. Both are rooted in the Messianic hope.

132

In Romans, Paul points out three very important facts.

First, some (not all) of the natural branches were broken off because of unbelief and the wild branches who believed were grafted in.

Second, the wild branches are nourished by the same sap from the root that also nourishes the natural branches. This life-giving sap comes from God, and the wild branches need to remember that the tree holds them up, not the other way around.

Third, the wild branches now in the tree better not be arrogant and boast against those natural branches that were broken off. Why? The natural branches can be grafted back in if they repent and believe. Furthermore, the punishment for the wild branches who dare to boast and become arrogant against the broken off natural branches is to risk being pruned off the tree by the Lord.

"If some of the branches have been broken off, and you, though a wild olive shoot, have been grafted in among the others and now share in the nourishing sap from the olive root, do not boast over those branches. If you do, consider this: You do not support the root, but the root supports you. You will say then, 'Branches were broken off so that I would be grafted in.' Granted. But, they were broken off because of unbelief, and you stand by faith. Do not be arrogant, but be afraid. For if God did not spare the natural branches, he will not spare you either. Consider therefore the kindness and sternness of God: sternness to those who fell, but kindness to you, provided that you continue in his kindness. Otherwise, you also will be cut off. And if they do not persist in unbelief, they will be grafted in, for God is able to graft them in again. After all, if you were cut out of an olive tree that is wild by nature, and contrary to nature were grafted into a cultivated olive tree, how much more readily will these, the natural branches, be grafted into their own olive tree!" (Rom. 11:17–24).

In an amazing and mysterious passage about God's covenant with His people Israel, Paul declares that God himself blinded them so that His gospel would be thrust out around the world, that we might be saved: "I do not want you to be ignorant of this mystery, brothers, so that you may not be conceited: Israel has experienced a hardening in part until the full number of Gentiles has come in" (Rom. 11:25).

133

134

When God desired to extend His covenants to the Gentile world through Jesus, this does not mean He was finished with His people Israel: "And, so all Israel will be saved, as it is written: 'The deliverer will come from

Zion; he will turn godlessness away from Jacob. And this is my covenant with them when I take away their sins' " (Rom. 11:26–27).

It was and is God's plan and desire that His  **135** church love and honor His people Israel for the fact that they travailed with God over the centuries, gave us the Bible, gave us our Savior, and brought salvation to us. If it had not been for them, we would still be heathens worshiping wood and stone idols. We have a debt to Israel. God's calling to them did not end 2,000 years ago, as His call is irrevocable.

"As far as the gospel is concerned, they are enemies on your account; but as far as election is concerned, they are loved on account of the patriarchs, for God's gifts and his call are irrevocable" (Rom 11:28–29).

 **136** Paul concludes that God's love can be extended to His covenant people Israel through the Church. He desires to show mercy to them. Then, speaking to the Church, Paul points out, "They too may now receive mercy as a result of God's mercy to you" (Rom. 11:31).

Christian love and mercy to **137**  Israel and the Jewish people extend beyond just prayer. Paul told us Gentile Christians that we also have a financial debt to pay to Israel and to help them meet their needs: "For if the Gentiles have shared in the Jews' spiritual blessings, they owe it to the Jews to share with them their material blessings" (Rom. 15:27).

138  In the language of the New Testament, we Gentile Christians have become spiritual Israel, but we did not take over the covenants of God with His people Israel, the Jewish people, who are the natural descendants of Abraham, Isaac, and Jacob.

We have become joint heirs (Gal. 3:29), brought near (Eph. 2:13) and grafted in (Rom. 11:17), but we did not take over — we joined into a covenant promise that started before us.

In the early centuries of the Christian Church, some church fathers began to teach that God had broken His covenants with the Jewish people and given them over to the Christians. These men developed a doctrine that is called "replacement theology," which claims that God signaled He was finished with Israel and the Jews when Herod's Temple was destroyed in A.D. 70. Many Jews were subsequently exiled from Jerusalem in A.D. 135 by the Roman emperor Hadrian. According to this teaching, which is still very prevalent

139

in the Church today, God bestowed all of the Bible's blessings on the Church, and all of His curses upon the Jews. This malevolent teaching has fueled much of Christian anti-Semitism and persecution of Jews by the Church throughout Christian history.

An ancient scroll of the Book of Esther.

140 Replacement theology is wrong, because the Jewish people did fulfill the Abrahamic promise to live in the land and be a witness for Him, to hear and record God's Word in the Bible, and bring forth the Messiah of the world — Jesus (Yeshua) — as a redemptive blessing to the whole world.

The gospel has gone around the world to bring the Gentiles closer to the God of Israel to fulfill His promise to Abraham that in him all the nations of the world would be blessed (Gen. 12:3). There was no reason for God to break or violate any of His promises or prophecies toward His covenant people, Israel. In fact, Romans 11 tells us that the Jewish people are "loved on account of the patriarchs" (v. 28) and that "they too may now receive mercy as a result of God's mercy to you" (v. 31).

Therefore, if God's covenant between His people and land, Israel, is unbreakable, then there must have been a plan to restore both as part of His blessing to the world. This restoration, which is occurring today, is setting the stage for the soon coming of the Messiah.

To support replacement theology, you 141 would have to believe God is denying His Word, His promises, and His covenants with Israel and the Jewish people. However, there is an easy test to prove that this is not so. In the New Testament, you need only to place the words "the Church," everywhere you find the word "Israel." Very quickly, you would see that it does not work.

For example, Romans 10:1 says, "Brothers, my heart's desire and prayer to God for the Israelites is that they may be saved." Now, if you replace the word "Israel" with the words "the Church," it would read that Paul's heart's desire is that "the Church might be saved." Well, the Church is saved, or else it would not be the Church. So, obviously, Paul is talking about God's covenant people, the Jewish people.

142  We Christians should be excited when we see God fulfilling His prophetic Word to His people, Israel, in keeping with His eternal covenants with them. This shows the faithfulness of God. After all, if He did not keep His promises to Israel, how could we really be sure He would keep His promises to the Church?

CHAPTER FOUR

JERUSALEM

143   I have lived in Jerusalem for over a quarter century, and I still get excited when I realize what a privilege it is to live in this special city. There is no other city like this on the face of the earth, because this is a city where so many important events of the Bible occurred.

King David summarizes the joy and excitement of coming "up to Jerusalem" to worship

Jerusalem, as viewed from the south.

the Most High God, the Lord God of Israel. "I rejoiced with those who said to me, 'Let us go to the house of the Lord.' Our feet are standing in your gates, O Jerusalem" (Ps. 122:1–2).

Over the centuries, Jerusalem has been **144** called by many names: Salem, the city of Melchizedek (Gen. 14:18; Heb. 7:1–2); Jebus, the city of the Jebusites that God commanded David to conquer for Him (1 Chron. 11:4); Jerusalem (*Yerushaliim*, in Hebrew), the City of Peace; the City of David (2 Sam. 6:10; 1 Kings. 2:10; 11:27; etc.); Aelia Capitolina, the Roman name given by Emperor Hadrian in A.D. 135; and El Kuds (the Holy), a name later given to this city by the Muslims.

Its Hebrew name, *Yerushaliim* (Josh. 10:1), ends with a plural form of shalom, the Hebrew word for "peace," indicating that it is not only the city of peace, but a city of a double portion of peace.

145 The name "Jerusalem" occurs 881 times in the Bible — 667 times in the Old Testament and 144 times in the New Testament.

Scholars say there are over 70 **146** different poetic and descriptive names for Jerusalem found in the Bible, with the most-used name being Zion (152 times) (1 Kings. 8:1; Zech. 9:13; etc.). Some of the many titles for Jerusalem are: the City of God (Ps. 46:4; 87:3); the City of Judah (2 Chron. 25:28); the City of Joy (Jer. 49:25); the City of Praise (Jer. 49:25); the City of Righteousness (Isa. 1:26); the City of the Great King (Ps. 48:2; Matt. 5:35); the City of the Lord (Isa. 60:14); the City of Truth (Zech. 8:3); the Faithful City (Isa. 1:26); the Gate of My People (Obad. 1:13; Mic. 1:9); Hephzibah and Beulah (Isa. 62:4); the Mountain of the Lord (Dan. 9:20; Zech. 8:3); the Perfection of Beauty (Lam. 2:15); Princess Among the Provinces (Lam. 1:1); the Throne of the Lord (Jer. 3:17); the Zion of the Holy One of Israel (Isa. 60:14), Ariel (lion of God) (Isa. 29:1).

147

God chose this city as His own and His claim is eternal and necessary for the outworking of His redemptive plan for the earth.

God himself refers to it and to no other place on earth as "My City" (Isa. 45:13) or more often, "My Holy Mountain" (Isa. 11:9; 56:7; 57:13; Ezek. 20:40; Joel 2:1; 3:17).

Because it is the City of God, where He has put His name, it is often referred to simply as the Holy City (Neh. 11:1, 18; Isa. 48:2; 52:1; Matt. 4:5; 27:53; Rev. 11:2).

God loves Jerusalem because it is His city which He chose for His dwelling place:

148

"He has set his foundation on the holy mountain; the LORD loves the gates of Zion more than all the dwellings of Jacob" (Ps. 87:1–2).

"For the LORD has chosen Zion, he has desired it for his dwelling: 'This is my resting place for ever and ever; here I will sit enthroned, for I have desired it — I will bless her with abundant provisions' " (Ps. 132:13–15).

149

How does the Bible describe Jerusalem? David said, "Jerusalem is built like a city that is closely compacted together" (Ps. 122:3). This aptly describes the physical appearance of Jerusalem even today . . . almost 3,000 years after

this psalm was written. Even today, if you look at the Old City from a distance, it becomes a two-dimensional patchwork of shapes and colors, as one building intertwines and is stacked upon another.

Jerusalem has been the main pilgrimage objective of devout men and women of faith for 3,000 years. "Many peoples will come and say, 'Come, let us go up to the mountain of the LORD, to the house of the God of Jacob. He will teach us his ways, so that we may walk in his paths' " (Isa. 2:3).

150

David also said that Jerusalem was the pilgrimage destination, "That is where the tribes go up, the tribes of the LORD, to praise the name of the LORD according to the statute given to Israel" (Ps. 122:4).

Even today, Jerusalem is a patchwork of buildings from different historical periods and also a patchwork of people, both residents and visitors alike. Here you can see Christian pilgrims from far-off lands, many in traditional native costumes; Hassidic Jews in their black tunics and knickers, fur hats, and side curls; and even a Bedouin from the desert riding into town on his camel to buy supplies.

151      In the days of the Bible, God specifically commanded His people, Israel, to "go up" to Jerusalem to celebrate the biblical feasts (Lev. 23) three times a year: at Passover, Shavuot (Pentecost), and Sukkot (Tabernacles). This had a great impact on the life of the capital — culturally, socially, and politically. Jews from all over the country and the world thronged to Jerusalem to bring their sacrifices, study the Torah, and rejoice. At the time of Jesus, the population of Jerusalem would swell to 250,000 people, about six times the normal population.

It is through these pilgrimage feasts that God reminded the people of what He had done for them (and us) throughout history. The purposes of celebrating these feasts is still the same today, and now both Jews and Christians come to Jerusalem at these feast times of the year to worship the Lord in Zion.

Worshipers in Jerusalem at the Feast of Tabernacles

152      Eventually, when the Lord returns, all nations will come up to Jerusalem to celebrate the Feast of Tabernacles with

Him: "Then the survivors from all the nations that have attacked Jerusalem will go up year after year to worship the King, the LORD Almighty, and to celebrate the Feast of Tabernacles" (Zech. 14:16).

153 The Psalmist further describes Jerusalem as "beautiful in its loftiness, the joy of the whole earth. Like the utmost heights of Zaphon is Mount Zion, the city of the Great King" (Ps. 48:2).

Jerusalem was and is a physical place where the presence of God dwells. The testimony of this city was a testimony of God coming to earth to redeem man. The Psalmist thought it worthy to tell this story from generation to generation: "Walk about Zion, go around her, count her towers, consider well her ramparts, view her citadels, that you may tell of them to the next generation. For this God is our God, for ever and ever; he will be our guide even to the end" (Ps. 48:12–14).

This Scripture is also for the millions of pilgrims who come to Jerusalem today and take God's message out to the world.

Psalm 125:1–2 says: "Those who trust in the 154 LORD are like Mount Zion, which cannot be shaken but endures for ever. As the mountains surround Jerusalem, so the LORD surrounds his people both now and for evermore."

Since Jerusalem sits on top of the central mountain range, how can the mountains surround Jerusalem? This can only be completely understood by seeing the location of the Old City of Jerusalem, which was located near to the Gihon Spring, which is found in the Kidron Valley and separates Jerusalem from the Mount of Olives on the east. To the west, there is modern-day Mount Zion, and to the north, the elevation is much higher than the biblical city. Therefore, even though Jerusalem is on the top of the mountain range along the watershed line, it is in a depression like a saucer, with higher ridges surrounding the city.

155   Like most large cities in the ancient world, Jerusalem was a walled city with gateways that could be closed at night or at times of war for protection. Since the gates of a city were the only way in or out of the city, the large doors of the gateway, which were made of metal and wood (Ps. 107:16; Isa. 45:2) were secured at night with iron or wooden cross bars (1 Kings. 4:13; Nah. 3:13) for the protection of the inhabitants.

The main gate of each city was large enough for the entry of chariots and carts. It was carefully designed and built

The Damascus Gate.

to deter the entrance of enemy soldiers, as this was the most vulnerable place in the walls of a city. The gates were often flanked by towers (2 Sam. 18:24, 33) on which watchmen stood, day and night.

We are called to be watchmen on the walls of Jerusalem to pray for this city to become a praise in the earth. "I have posted watchmen on your walls, O Jerusalem; they will never be silent day or night. You who call on the LORD, give yourselves no rest, and give him no rest until he establishes Jerusalem and makes her the praise of the earth (Isa. 62:6–7).

The city gate was the busiest place in the city. Near or just inside the gates there were courtyards or broadenings of the street where much of the city's social, business, and legal interaction took place.

156

Here is where we find the reading of the law and proclamations taking place (Josh. 20:4; 2 Chron. 32:6; Neh. 8:1, 3); where justice was administered as the elders judged legal cases and business transactions (Deut. 16:18; 2 Sam. 15:2, Amos 5:10–15); where news was exchanged and discussed (Gen. 19:1); and local gossip was spread (Ps. 69:12). It was a place where markets flourished (e.g., the Fish Gate [Neh. 3:3], the Sheep Gate [Neh. 3:1], the Water Gate [Neh. 3:26], the Horse Gate [Neh. 3:28] in Jerusalem), and where trading centers for imported items (Isa. 3:18–24) were established.

Prophets and priests delivered admonitions and pronouncements at the gates (Isa. 29:21; Amos 5:10; Jer. 17:19; etc.). Criminals were punished just outside the gates (1 Kings 21:10; Acts 7:58). The city gate was even the place where one could attract the attention of the sovereign or dignitary (2 Sam 19:8; 1 Kings 22:10; Esther 2:19, 21; 3:2). It was where strangers who were visiting the city passed the night, if they had no place to stay.

To be chosen as an elder to sit at the gate of the city was an honorable position (Prov. 31:23; Dan. 2:49), although it became a curse for Lot who chose to be an elder at the gate of Sodom where he compromised his stand for the Lord (Gen. 19:1).

157   Today, there are nine gateways into the walls of the Old City of Jerusalem. On the northern wall, there is the New Gate, the ancient Damascus Gate, and Herod's Gate. On the eastern wall, there is the Lion's Gate, also known as St. Stephen's Gate, and the Eastern or Golden Gate which was sealed up by the Muslims in the 16th century to prevent the Messiah (Jesus) from entering to the Temple Mount as predicted by the prophets. On the southern wall, there is the Dung Gate and Zion Gate, and now the recently reopened Tanner's Gate that was closed centuries ago. On the western wall there is only the main Jaffa Gate.

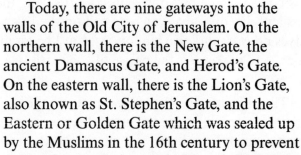

Jerusalem has always been central to God's 158
redemptive plan for the world. The Bible records the event when the Lord gave Jerusalem into the hands of King David in 1004 B.C.: "David and all the Israelites marched to Jerusalem (that is, Jebus). The Jebusites who lived there said to David, 'You will not get in here.' Nevertheless, David captured the fortress of Zion, the City of David. . . . David then took up residence in the fortress, and so it was called the City of David. He built up the city around it, from the supporting terraces to the surrounding wall, while Joab restored the rest of the city. And David became more and more powerful, because the LORD Almighty was with him" (1 Chron. 11:4–9).

159   David conquered the city with God's blessing because God chose the site. It was located on the border between Judah and Benjamin and was a bridge between Israel and Judah to bring the tribes together. Jerusalem became both the spiritual and administrative capital of Israel, a position it still holds today. From here, the king ruled, and God's presence dwelled in His temple where He was worshiped. As such, the die was cast for Jerusalem, the City of Peace, to be central in world events.

It was of paramount importance to God   160
that David establish Jerusalem as the site of
God's holy temple, where His presence would
dwell:

"But now I have chosen Jerusalem for my Name to be there, and I have chosen David to rule my people Israel" (2 Chron. 6:6).

"I will defend this city and save it, for my sake and for the sake of David my servant" (2 Kings 19:34).

"Nevertheless, for David's sake the LORD his God gave him a lamp in Jerusalem by raising up a son to succeed him and by making Jerusalem strong" (1 Kings 15:4).

161   David bought the threshing floor of Araunah for an altar for the Lord (2 Sam. 24) and ultimately brought the ark of the Lord to Jerusalem (1 Chron. 15). On this site, Solomon built the glorious first temple (1 Chron. 3:1), and it was also the site of the second temple, embellished to incomparable grandeur by King Herod.

Model of the ancient Temple of the God
of Israel in Jerusalem.

It was on the Temple Mount site that God's 162
presence dwelled in Jerusalem for over a thousand years, and it is to this place that the Lord
will return to establish His millennial kingdom
in Israel. He will rule and reign in the earth,
from Jerusalem.

163 The law of God and Word of
the Lord were to emanate from Jerusalem:
"The law will go out from Zion, the word
of the LORD from Jerusalem" (Isa. 2:3).
"May the LORD bless you from Zion all the
days of your life; may you see the prosperity of
Jerusalem" (Ps. 128:5).

164

In the Bible, the temple site came to be
known as Mount Zion, and later as Mount
Moriah, the place where Abraham took Isaac
for sacrifice. Today's Mount Zion is outside the

southwest corner of the Old City walls, located on the Western Hill. This area was inside the walls of Herod's second temple-period city. One thousand years after King David, his small city had grown quite large.

Today, we find on the Temple Mount two Muslim mosques, and the area is completely controlled by the Muslim authorities. Jews and Christians are not allowed to pray at this site, and if they do, they are removed by the Muslim authorities.

165

Nevertheless, no matter what the Muslims say, no matter what the United Nations, the Palestinian Authority, or anybody else says, the Jewish people still own this Temple Mount. David bought it (2 Sam. 24), it has been recorded for all time, and the deed is still valid.

166

In the fulfillment of Bible prophecy, the Jewish people have come back into this land by the millions.

However, today, instead of worshiping the Lord on the Temple Mount, they are praying at only a small section of an outer retaining wall of the Temple Mount built by King Herod — known as the Western Wall.

Jews praying at the Western Wall

Many Christians and Jews today believe   167
that a day is coming when the God of the Bible
will be honored on top of the Temple Mount
again. From here, the Lord will be worshiped in
a third temple that is yet to be built on the site.
The Messiah will rule and reign from Jerusalem, and the nations will stream up to worship
Him (Zech. 14:16). When and how this will occur, only God knows. Meanwhile, this place that once was a
lowly threshing floor remains a place of utmost importance
even in this prophetic day, as all of history is becoming
increasingly focused on Israel and Jerusalem.

168   When King David died, ". . . he was buried
in the City of David" (1 Kings 2:10). This was
very unusual, because the Jews were forbidden
from having cemeteries within the city walls,
due to the prohibition of touching the dead.
However, David was so loved that he was ap-
parently placed in a special tomb in his honor.
        While there are at least two possible locations
suggested by archaeologists, no one really knows where he
is buried. The traditional Tomb of David, which everyone
visits, is located on the present-day Mount Zion, or the
Western Hill, which was not part of the City of David during David's time.

Because God chose Jerusalem as His own   169
and decided that it would be the administrative and political capital of Israel and the religious focal point of the Jewish people, nations
have both revered and reviled this most unique
city throughout history. It has been fought
over by more people from more nations than
any other city on earth. Because it is God's

city, Jerusalem has played a role in history out of all proportion to its economic importance, location, or size.

170

It has been estimated that between 50,000 and 60,000 books have been written about Jerusalem and 6,000 maps have been printed in the last 700 years. Both attest to its centrality in the focus of the world. However, despite the apparent importance of Jerusalem to the Arab, Muslim world, no Arab maps of the Holy City have been found.[1]

Paradoxically, Jerusalem, the City of Peace, has known more sieges and battles than any other city in history. According to the conventional records, Jerusalem underwent 37 conquests. In fact, the city has changed hands 86 times, including many minor conquests.[2]

171

From the time of Melchizedek and Abraham, Jerusalem underwent major conquests by the Amorites, Joshua, the Jebusites, David — for the Lord, the Philistines, Babylonians, Assyrians, Macedonians, Ptolemies, Seleucids, Romans, Byzantines, Persians, Arabs, Seljuks, Crusaders, Mongols, Mamelukes, Turks, British, Jordanians, and now Israel is back once again.

172

Jerusalem was the royal city, the capital of the only kingdom God has established among men; here His temple was erected, and here alone were sacrifices legitimately offered to the Lord.

173

At a time when the people of Israel were in the Babylonian exile, God yearned for them to return and rebuild

His beloved Jerusalem: "This is what the LORD Almighty says: 'I am very jealous for Jerusalem and Zion, but I am very angry with the nations that feel secure. I was only a little angry, but they added to the calamity.' Therefore, this is what the LORD says: 'I will return to Jerusalem with mercy, and there my house will be rebuilt. And the measuring line will be stretched out over Jerusalem,' declares the LORD Almighty. Proclaim further: This is what the LORD Almighty says: 'My towns will again overflow with prosperity, and the LORD will again comfort Zion and choose Jerusalem' " (Zech. 1:14–17).

174  The second temple, or Herod's Temple, was one of the wonders of the ancient world. According to Josephus (A.D. 37–93), 10,000 building laborers were employed in the construction and 1,000 chariots were needed to bring up the building materials. It took eight years to build.

The Romans destroyed this temple in A.D. 70, leaving only the western portion of the outer retaining wall of the platform on which it was built. This was done to remind the Jews and the world of both the magnificence of the temple and the totality of their destruction. Most of the stones average 42 inches in height (106 cm), and 10 feet in length (305 cm). Some are as long as 39 feet (12 m) in length and weigh over 100 tons. In the middle of the wall, the largest stone is 42 feet (13 m) x 14 feet (4 m) x 11 feet (3 m) and weighs 400 tons! They are all beautifully cut with smooth surfaces and beveled edges. No mortar was used to build a wall over 70 feet (21 m) in height.

175

176  For Jews around the world, there is the custom of leaving part of a wall in one's house unfinished or unpainted, called *Zecher la Hurban*, which is to always remind them of the destruction of the temple. On the ninth of the Hebrew month of Av (August), Jews remember the destruction of both the first and second temples. Both acts show how the Jewish people are still closely tied to this holy city.

Politically, Jerusalem has been a capital city to no other nation in history except Israel and the Jewish people. In fact, past efforts of other nations to conquer Jerusalem have been because it was so important to the Jewish people and was the focus of the Jews' religious and political aspirations. 177

178  Christianity and Islam centralized the importance of Jerusalem because of biblical events that were a part of the life of Israel and the Jewish people that were later appropriated by each faith. Granted, Christianity has a direct connection to Jerusalem. However, the connection involves the life, death, resurrection, and soon return of Jesus, who was Jewish, and whose mission was in context with God's redemptive plan for Israel, as well as the rest of the world.

179
For Islam, Jerusalem is never mentioned in the Koran. The Muslims connect their tie to the city based on the legendary night ride through the heavens by Mohammed on his winged horse, Barak, which took him from "the sacred mosque" to the "farthest mosque."

According to the Koran, the journey occurred in the prophet's dream in a split second. The Muslims say that this "farthest mosque" is Jerusalem, even though Jerusalem is not specifically mentioned. After the stopover at the "farthest" mosque, Mohammed is said to have arrived at the seventh heaven, where he was met by Abraham, Isaac, Joseph, Moses, and Jesus and received their blessing to become the last prophet of God. In actuality, Mohammed never set foot in Jerusalem as he died in A.D. 632, six years before Caliph Omar conquered the city in 639. Islam's claim to the Temple Mount rests on this legend alone.

180  In early Islamic history, which incorporated some ideas from Judaism and Christianity, the people prayed facing Jerusalem. However, once Mohammed saw that the Jews of the Middle East would not accept his new religion, the direction of Muslim prayer turned away from Jerusalem and toward Mecca.

The noted Arab geographer Yakkut, in his voluminous lexicon (A.D. 1225), referred to Jerusalem as "holy to Jews and Christians," but described Mecca as sacred to Muslims.

Today, Jerusalem is referred to as the third 181 most holy site in Islam and the world is led to believe that the city needs to be shared with the Muslim world because it is so important to them. However, at first, Islam did not consider Jerusalem to be holy to Islam, calling the city *Bayt al-Muqaddas*, from the Hebrew *Beit Hamikdash* (the Temple). Ceremonies at the Dome of the Rock, built in A.D. 692 on the Temple Mount, were held on Mondays and Thursdays (holy weekdays for the Jews), not Friday which is holy to Muslims. These services were attended by Jews, and incorporated Jewish worship practices, not Islamic practices.

Islamic writings, called *Hadiths*, praising Jerusalem in relation to Islam, were only compiled in A.D. 1019. Hadiths in praise of Mecca, Medina, Damascus, and Baghdad had been published much earlier, indicating that the sanctity of Jerusalem in Islam was of a much later date. Also, Islam never considered Jerusalem as a capital city. Islamic rulers of Israel (Palestine), i.e., the Arabs, Seljuks, Mamelukes, and Turks, spanning nearly a millennia of control in total, established their administrative center on the coastal plains in a city they built, called Ramle, not Jerusalem.

182

Geographically, Jerusalem lacks everything that made other great cities important and great. It has no waterways, it was located off the main trade routes, and it has no strategic importance to a conquering army. What Jerusalem did have is that it was and is the God-given spiritual and administrative center of Israel.

Jerusalem was the city of the prophets of the Bible, as well as the kings of David's line — the kings of Judah.

183

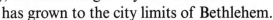

Jesus, of the line of David, was born in Bethlehem (Beit Lechem, House of Bread, in Hebrew), which is only five miles south of Jerusalem. Today, the much larger city of Jerusalem has grown to the city limits of Bethlehem.

184

In Jerusalem occurred the death, resurrection, and ascension of Jesus Christ (the Messiah), and to Jerusalem He will return. Jesus knew of the fate that awaited Him in Jerusalem, but that it was part of the Father's plan for the redemption of the world. "From that time on Jesus began to explain to his disciples that he must go to Jerusalem and suffer many things at the hands of the elders, chief priests and teachers of the law, and that he must be killed and on the third day be raised to life" (Matt. 16:21).

"They were on their way up to Jerusalem, with Jesus leading the way. . . . Again he took the Twelve aside and told them what was going to happen to him. 'We are going up to Jerusalem,' he said, 'and the Son of Man will be betrayed to the chief priests and teachers of the law. They will condemn him to death and will hand him over to the Gentiles, who will mock him and spit on him, flog him and kill him. Three days later he will rise" (Mark 10:32–34). Note that it was the Gentiles who killed Him, not the Jews.

The Mount of Olives was called this because of its groves of olive trees. During the

185

time of Jesus, olive oil was the only food product exported from the Jerusalem area. This mountain is where Jesus and His disciples stayed when they came to Jerusalem. Bethany, where Martha, Mary, and Lazarus lived, is on the eastern face. On the western slope, facing the Temple Mount, which is separated by the Kidron Valley, are the olive groves where Jesus spent time with His disciples, made His

Ancient olive trees, like this one, grow in the Garden of Gethsemane.

triumphal entry on a colt, wept over the city, and prayed before His arrest.

At the base of the Mount of Olives is the Garden of Gethsemane, where Jesus agonized in prayer to the Father before His arrest. The root stock of the olive trees in this garden are said to be over 2,000 years old and would have witnessed Jesus' prayers.

186   Jesus will come again, just as He promised. The prophet Zechariah predicted this event, and the angels of the Lord confirmed this at His ascension from the top of the Mount.

"On that day his feet will stand on the Mount of Olives, east of Jerusalem, and the Mount of Olives will be split in two from east to west, forming a great valley, with half of the mountain moving north and half moving south" (Zech. 14:4).

"After he said this, he was taken up before their very eyes, and a cloud hid him from their sight. They were looking intently up into the sky as he was going, when suddenly two men dressed in white stood beside them. 'Men of Galilee,' they said, 'why do you stand here looking into the sky? This same Jesus, who has been taken from you into heaven, will come back in the same way you have seen him go into heaven.' Then they returned to Jerusalem from the hill called the Mount of Olives, a Sabbath day's walk from the city" (Acts 1:9–12).

God's deliverer would come into and out of   187 Zion for the whole House of Israel, and ultimately for the world:

" 'The Redeemer will come to Zion, to those in Jacob who repent of their sins,' declares the LORD" (Isa. 59:20).

"And so all Israel will be saved, as it is written: 'The deliverer will come from Zion; he will turn godlessness away from Jacob. And this is my covenant with them when I take away their sins' " (Rom. 11:26–27).

"And everyone who calls on the name of the Lord will be saved; for on Mount Zion and in Jerusalem there will be deliverance, as the Lord has said, among the survivors whom the Lord calls" (Joel 2:32).

188  Isaiah says that the Lord would lay a foundation stone in Jerusalem, which Paul confirms is Jesus, the Messiah, whom the Gentiles pursued and found:

"So this is what the Sovereign Lord says: 'See, I lay a stone in Zion, a tested stone, a precious cornerstone for a sure foundation; the one who trusts will never be dismayed' " (Isa. 28:16).

"The Lord Almighty is the one you are to regard as holy . . . he will be a stone that causes men to stumble and a rock that makes them fall. And for the people of Jerusalem he will be a trap and a snare" (Isa. 8:13–14).

"See, I lay in Zion a stone that causes men to stumble and a rock that makes them fall, and the one who trusts in him will never be put to shame" (Rom. 9:33).

While many people did recognize Jesus as the Messiah, most of the leaders in Jerusalem did not. Therefore, Jesus wept over this city and prophesied a day when the people would recognize Him: "O Jerusalem, Jerusalem, you who kill the prophets and stone those sent to you, how often I have longed to gather your children together, as a hen gathers her chicks under her wings, but you were not willing. Look, your house is left to you desolate. For I tell you, you will not see me again until 189

you say, 'Blessed is he who comes in the name of the Lord' "
(Matt.23:37–39).

190  The Great Commission to take the gospel
to the world was to begin in Jerusalem, spread
to the surrounding regions, and then the world:
"Then Jesus came to them [His disciples]
and said, 'All authority in heaven and on earth
has been given to me. Therefore go and make
disciples of all nations, baptizing them in the
name of the Father and of the Son and of the
Holy Spirit, and teaching them to obey everything I have
commanded you. And surely I am with you always, to the
very end of the age' " (Matt. 28:18–20).

"He told them, 'This is what is written: The Christ [Messiah] will suffer and rise from the dead on the third day, and repentance and forgiveness of sins will be preached in his name
to all nations, beginning at Jerusalem' " (Luke 24:46–47).

"But you will receive power when the Holy Spirit comes
on you; and you will be my witnesses in Jerusalem, and in all
Judea and Samaria, and to the ends of the earth" (Acts 1:8).

The Holy Spirit descended upon an assem-   191
bled group in Jerusalem at Pentecost (Shavuot),
giving birth to the Church (Acts 2), and here the
first great Church Council was held (Acts 15).

192  No site in all the Scriptures
received such constant and ex-
alted praise as Jerusalem. No
other place in the world has had such promises
made of ultimate glory and permanent peace.
God's everlasting exhortation to His people is
to "Pray for the peace of Jerusalem: 'May they
prosper who love you' " (Ps. 122:6; NASB).

Jerusalem is eternal, according to the Lord:
"Then kings who sit on David's throne will
come through the gates of this city with their
officials. They and their officials will come
riding in chariots and on horses, accompanied
by the men of Judah and those living in Jerusalem, and this city will be inhabited for ever"
(Jer. 17:25).

"Those who trust in the LORD are like Mount Zion,
which cannot be shaken, but endures forever" (Ps. 125:1).

 God has a special blessing for people born
in Jerusalem: "Indeed, of Zion it will be said,
'This one and that one were born in her, and
the Most High himself will establish her.' The
LORD will write in the register of the peoples:
'This one was born in Zion' " (Ps. 87:5–6).

The Jewish sages of old declared that "of
ten measures of beauty that came into the
world, nine were given to Jerusalem and one to
the rest of the world." Such love for a place is
unsurpassed.

The Psalmist agrees: "From Zion, perfect in
beauty, God shines forth" (Ps. 50:2).

 The Roman historian Pliny, of the first cen-
tury, referred to Jerusalem as "by far the most
famous city of the ancient Orient."

George Adam Smith has said, "Jerusalem
felt God's presence. She was assured of His
love and as never another city on earth has
been, of God's travail for her worthiness of the
destiny to which He had called her."

God and the Jewish people never forgot **197**
their holy city, Jerusalem. This connection was
part of God's divine, covenantal, and sovereign
will for this special city.

Isaiah wrote God's feelings for Jerusalem:
"But Zion said, 'The LORD has forsaken me,
the Lord has forgotten me. Can a mother forget
the baby at her breast and have no compassion
on the child she has borne? Though she may forget, I will
not forget you! See, I have engraved you on the palms of my
hands; your walls are ever before me' " (Isa. 49:14–16).

The Psalmist declared boldly: "If I forget you, O Jerusalem, may my right hand forget its skill. May my tongue cling
to the roof of my mouth if I do not remember you, if I do
not consider Jerusalem my highest joy" (Ps. 137:5–6).

198 Teddy Kollek, Jerusalem's beloved former
mayor, said, "For three thousand years, Jerusalem has been the center of Jewish hope
and longing. No other city has played such a
dominant role in the history, culture, religion,
and consciousness of a people as has Jerusalem
in the life of Jewry and Judaism. Throughout
centuries of exile, Jerusalem remained alive in
the hearts of Jews everywhere as the focal point of Jewish
history, the symbol of ancient glory, spiritual fulfillment,
and modern renewal. This heart and soul of the Jewish
people engenders the thought that if you want one simple
word to symbolize all of Jewish history, that
word would be 'Jerusalem.' "[3] **199**

Every year at Passover, Jewish people who
live outside of Israel will recite the vow, "Next
year in Jerusalem," indicating their desire to eat
the Passover in Jerusalem.

In the Amidah, the silent part of the Jewish prayer, they pray, "May our eyes behold Your return to Zion in mercy."

In grace after meals, Jews pray that the Almighty may "rebuild Jerusalem speedily in our days."[4]

Three times a day for thousands of years, Jews have prayed, "To Jerusalem, Thy city, shall we return with joy."

200 After the time of David's conquest, Jerusalem was inhabited by the Jewish people until the Babylonian captivity (586 B.C.). However, under Ezra and Nehemiah they returned to rebuild Jerusalem and remained there in greater and lesser numbers until the great exiles of the Romans in A.D. 70 and A.D. 135. There has always been a remnant, but Jews were not a religious majority in Jerusalem again until 1818.

201 Since 1818, the Jewish population has been the religious majority in Jerusalem. Today, over 70 percent of Jerusalem's 700,000 residents are Jewish. Jerusalem, a dusty forgotten city with less than 15,000 inhabitants at the beginning of the 1800s, is once again the focus of the world's attention. During Jerusalem's past 3,000 years of history, the population figures attest to the fact that the number of inhabitants flourished under Jewish and Christian rule, but declined under Muslim rule.[5]

610 B.C., Jewish rule prior to Babylonian conquest — 20,000

A.D. 10, Jewish rule under Herod — 35,000

65, Jewish rule on eve of Roman conquest — 50,000

638, Christian rule under the Byzantines — 60,000

1050, Fatimid Muslim rule — 20,000

1180, Crusader Christian rule — 30,000

1450, Mamluk Muslim rule — 10,000

1690, Early Turkish (Ottoman) Muslim rule — 10,000
1800, Mid-Ottoman rule — 12,000
1910, Late Ottoman rule with Jewish immigration —
       75,000
1946, Late British Mandate (Christian rule) — 165,000
1967, Unification of Jerusalem (Jewish rule) —
       250,000
2003, Israeli census (Jewish rule) — 705,000

202

Although Jerusalem was in Muslim hands
for nearly 1,200 years (interrupted only by the
short period of the Crusader kingdom), most
of the time the rulers were non-Arab Muslims,
such as the Fatimids, Seljuks, Mamluks, and
Ottoman Turks. The decline in population
under Muslim rule shows the insignificant role
Jerusalem played in Muslim eyes.

From 1948–1967, when eastern Jerusalem   203
was in Jordanian Muslim hands and Jews were
not allowed to enter, only one Muslim leader
visited the city that is supposed to be so holy to
the Muslims. This leader was King Abdullah
I of Jordan, great-grandfather of the current
King Abdullah II. He was shot and killed in
1953 on his visit to Jerusalem outside the Al
Aksa Mosque by a Palestinian Arab.

204

The prophets foretold of the centrality of
Jerusalem at the end of days, when the eyes of
the world would be focused on this city (Zech.
2:1–5; 8:15; 12:2–3). Today, there is almost
daily press reporting about this tiny nation.
In Jerusalem, even an offhanded comment
by a politician or the building of a residential

neighborhood can become the stuff of a U.N. Security Council debate.

Psalms 102:13–14 says, "You will arise and have compassion on Zion, for it is time to show favour to her; the appointed time has come. For her stones are dear to your servants; her very dust moves them to pity." Since the city has been reunited, an unparalleled renovation effort has been underway by the Jewish people to restore the city to its former glory as the capital of the nation of Israel.

205

The Jewish people have even removed the dust from the ancient stones as the archaeologists have uncovered evidence of Jerusalem's glorious past. Yes, the time to favor Zion is now.

206

Since 1967 and the Six-Day War when Jordan attacked Israel, Israel became sovereign over all of Jerusalem, including the Temple Mount and the biblical Old City. Today, after about 1,900 years of exile, we can celebrate with the Jewish people the fulfillment of God's prophetic plan for Jerusalem, as He sets the stage for the coming of the Messiah.

In Luke 21, Jesus spoke of prophetic events that would occur just before His return. Of Jerusalem, He said, "Jerusalem will be trampled on by the Gentiles until the times of the Gentiles are fulfilled" (Luke 21:24).

Many Bible scholars believe that the reunification of Jerusalem in 1967 was a fulfillment of Luke 21:24. Is it any surprise that the sovereignty of Jerusalem is now being challenged by the Palestinian Authority, which is claiming the Old City and eastern sectors (biblical Jerusalem) as its capital, and for Islam?

Many Christians and Jews share a biblical view of united Jerusalem under Jewish sovereignty as a fulfillment of Bible prophecy. The New Testament speaks of Jerusalem and Israel as the place that Jesus will return, not Palestine or El-Kuds, the Muslim name for Israel and Jerusalem. Jesus is not returning to a Muslim country or capital city, but to one that is united and ruled by His people, the Jewish people, who are the covenant heirs of the promises to Abraham, Isaac, and Jacob. However, most people around the world see united Jerusalem under Jewish sovereignty as an obstacle to peace and are ready to divide it.

207

208

In our lifetime, Jerusalem has grown and expanded to its most magnificent size and beauty in history. God has truly worked to fulfill His prophetic Word. The stage is now set for the coming of the Lord and the building up of Jerusalem is another of the keys of His return. Today, there are some 2,000 synagogues, churches, mosques and other religious edifices in Jerusalem.[6] "For the LORD will rebuild Zion and appear in his glory" (Ps. 102:16).

In 1975, the U.N. General Assembly adopted a resolution equating Zionism with racism. This was orchestrated by the Arab and Communist blocs within the United Nations. Fortunately, with the breakdown of the Soviet Union and pressure from Western nations, this resolution was rescinded in 1991, although many Arab and Muslim countries voted against the repeal. What does the word "Zionism" mean? Simply, Zionism is derived from the word Zion, the traditional synonym for Jerusalem

209

An ever-growing, modern Jerusalem.

and the land of Israel. Zionism is the movement to re-establish the Jewish people in their ancestral homeland and is rooted in the continuous longing and deep attachment to the land of Israel. Christians who support God's prophetic plan for the return of the Jews to Israel in fulfillment of God's Word are called Christian Zionists.

So central is this desire to return to Jerusalem (Zion), when the Ethiopian Jews came to Israel from Ethiopia, for many, the only two words of Hebrew they knew were, "Yerushaliim" and "shalom. "

210

In 1996, Jerusalem celebrated 3,000 years since David made it the capital of Israel. Even though Jerusalem was occupied by Gentile nations since the days of the Romans, this is no longer the case.

You would think that the nations of the world would be rejoicing that God is fulfilling His prophetic plans for Jerusalem, but this is not so! While artists, musicians, actors, writers, and a host of ordinary pilgrims visit the city to show their solidarity with Israel, the politicians of the world avoid any such support of Jerusalem as the capital of Israel. Even U.S. presidents who have pledged to move the U.S. Embassy from Tel Aviv to Jerusalem as a campaign platform, have always reneged on this pledge. Even when the U.S. Congress mandated the move of the U.S. Embassy by an almost unanimous vote, U.S. presidents keep postponing its construction in Jerusalem in deference to the Muslim nations who are against it.

211

Like the false mother who stood before Solomon, some world leaders would prefer to cut the city of Jerusalem in two and give the biblical half to the Palestinians, instead of upholding the historical right of the Jewish people and the nation of Israel to the undivided city God gave to them. The idea of dividing Jerusalem into two capitals was unspeakable at one time. Now, the politicians and journalists are concerning themselves with the questions of "when," not the question of "if."

212

Man didn't choose Jerusalem, God did! He will judge the nations of the world who do not uphold His prophetic will for Jerusalem: "For the LORD has a day of vengeance, a year of retribution, to uphold Zion's cause" (Isa. 34:8). The King James Version of the Bible speaks of God judging the nations "for the controversy of Zion."

God will have the last word upon the nations **213**
of the world who don't support His prophetic
plan for Jerusalem. In Zechariah 12, God foretold a day of judgment against the nations who
come against Jerusalem, just before the coming
of the Messiah. Listen to what He says: "I am
going to make Jerusalem a cup that sends all the
surrounding peoples reeling. Judah will be besieged as well as Jerusalem. On that day, when all the nations
of the earth are gathered against her, I will make Jerusalem
an immovable rock for all the nations. All who try to move it
will injure themselves. . . . On that day I will set out to destroy all the nations that attack Jerusalem" (Zech. 12:2–9).

Just as God used Jerusalem and Israel as a standard in
days of old to determine if nations understood and supported His agenda for the world, today He is again using a
regathered Israel and the city of Jerusalem, now the capital
of a re-established Jewish state, as a prophetic test. Sadly,
most world leaders are more intent on gaining increased
influence, power, and wealth as part of a New World Order,
and are distancing themselves from what they see as "out-
dated" Bible passages and promises.

214  The trumpet is again sounding in Jerusalem. God's call to all people and nations to
follow Him and His eternal program may soon
end abruptly in judgment upon those who
choose to ignore it (Ps. 83). Regardless of the
efforts of the nations of the world and the New
World Order to dislocate Israel's covenantal,
God-given right to this city, Bible-believers
need to maintain their own strong stand in opposition to
this effort. Granted, you won't be very popular for this
stand, but no one who has stood boldly for biblical posi-
tions has been very popular in our world system.

Regardless of the efforts to re-divide Jerusalem, we need to maintain our own strong stand in favor of God's prophetic plan to prepare this city for the coming of the Messiah. Naturally, we can expect the world to oppose this.

Psalm 122:6 tells us to "Pray for the peace **215** of Jerusalem," recognizing that what we are praying for is God's peace that will come according to His plan. Lydia Prince, in her book *Appointment in Jerusalem*, saw the earth with one God-appointed center: JERUSALEM. Out from its center in divine plan, truth and peace were to flow to all lands; to it would return the worship and offerings of the nations. The outworking of prayer for Jerusalem would bless all lands and all peoples. Actually, the peace of the whole world depends upon the peace of Jerusalem. In the fulfillment of this plan lies earth's only hope.

216 Each Bible-believer is called to be a watchman on the walls of Jerusalem. The Book of Isaiah reminds all people who pray to the God of the Bible, the Lord God of Israel, to continually intercede for Zion: "For Zion's sake I will not keep silent, for Jerusalem's sake I will not remain quiet, till her righteousness shines out like the dawn, her salvation like a blazing torch. . . . I have posted watchmen on your walls, O Jerusalem; they will never be silent day or night. You who call on the LORD, give yourselves no rest, and give him no rest till he establishes Jerusalem and makes her the praise of the earth" (Isa. 62:1–7).

Yes, Jerusalem is the City of God, and she will only find her true peace and be a praise in the earth as His prophetic Word is fulfilled.

Bible-believers are exhorted to comfort and
bless Jerusalem:

"Comfort, comfort my people, says your
God. Speak tenderly to Jerusalem, and proclaim to her that her hard service has been
completed, that her sin has been paid for, that
she has received from the LORD's hand double
for all her sins" (Isa. 40:1–2).

"In your good pleasure make Zion prosper; build up the
walls of Jerusalem" (Ps. 51:18).

"Rejoice with Jerusalem and be glad for her, all you who
love her; rejoice greatly with her, all you who mourn over
her" (Isa. 66:10).

218   In a day to come, there will be a new Jerusalem: "Then I saw a new heaven and a new
earth, for the first heaven and the first earth
had passed away, and there was no longer any
sea. I saw the Holy City, the new Jerusalem,
coming down out of heaven from God, prepared as a bride beautifully dressed for her
husband" (Rev. 21:1–2).

God promises future blessing on Jerusalem:

"But be glad and rejoice for ever in what I will
create, for I will create Jerusalem to be a delight
and its people a joy. I will rejoice over Jerusalem and take delight in my people; the sound
of weeping and of crying will be heard in it no
more" (Isa. 65:18–19)

"The LORD will surely comfort Zion and
will look with compassion on all her ruins; he will make
her deserts like Eden, her wastelands like the garden of the
LORD. Joy and gladness will be found in her, thanksgiving
and the sound of singing" (Isa. 51:3).

220

The new Jerusalem will be magnificent:

"And he carried me away in the Spirit to a mountain great and high, and showed me the Holy City, Jerusalem, coming down out of heaven from God. It shone with the glory of God, and its brilliance was like that of a very precious jewel, like a jasper, clear as crystal. It had a great, high wall with twelve gates, and with twelve angels at the gates. On the gates were written the names of the twelve tribes of Israel" (Rev. 21:10–12).

"The wall was made of jasper, and the city of pure gold, as pure as glass. The foundations of the city walls were decorated with every kind of precious stone" (Rev. 21:18–19).

"The twelve gates were twelve pearls, each gate made of a single pearl. The great street of the city was of pure gold, like transparent glass" (Rev. 21:21).

Note that God still honors His covenant with the city and His people, Israel, as the gates of the city are named for the 12 tribes of Israel.

There will be no temple in this new Jerusalem because God and the Lamb who dwell there are the temple and its source of light: "I did not see a temple in the city, because the Lord God Almighty and the Lamb are its temple. The city does not need the sun or the moon to shine on it, for the glory of God gives it light, and the Lamb is its lamp. The nations will walk by its light, and the kings of the earth will bring their splendour into it" (Rev. 21:22–24).

221

222

The new Jerusalem will be a holy and open city to receive the nations of the world who will come to pay homage and to worship the Lord: "On no day will its gates ever be shut, for there will be no night there. The glory and honour of the nations will be brought into it. Nothing impure will ever enter it, nor will anyone who does what is shameful or deceitful, but only those whose names are written in the Lamb's book of life" (Rev. 21:25–27).

CHAPTER FIVE

ISRAEL IN PROPHECY

223

God chose Israel and the Jewish people to be His instruments on earth to bring salvation to the world. Because of these faithful covenant people, God showed the world the blessedness of serving the one true God, gave us His Word in the Bible, gave us His Messiah, and gave us the gift of salvation. All of this took place in the land of Israel.

The covenantal relationship between God and Israel did not end after the death and resurrection of Jesus and the destruction of the second temple. Not only did God relate through His people and land in the days of the Bible, but also the prophets spoke forth the clear message of God. Before the second coming of the Lord, the Messiah, God would manifest himself through Israel again. He is doing this to prepare for the messianic arrival and to show the world that He is a covenant-keeping God, faithful to His Word (Ezek. 36:33–36).

224

This is that day! In fact, you can say we are living in the "Days of the Bible" once again. In my organization, Bridges for Peace, we have a slogan related to our outreach projects in Israel that says: "Why just read about Bible prophecy when you can be a part of it!" God is moving His hand on behalf of Israel and the Jewish people today, and many Christians have recognized this and have become very active in the current outworking of God's prophetic Word today.

225  God has never broken His covenant concerning the Jewish people and the land. He is not finished blessing the world through these people from the land He called His own.

God never had a Plan A for the Jewish people and a Plan B for the Gentile church. He has only had a Plan A for the redemption of the world. We, as a Church, were brought into God's ongoing redemptive process (Eph. 2:11–13; Rom. 11:11–32), which is still connected to the land of Israel.

Sadly, the world and spiritual forces have fought God's plans throughout the ages.

Nearly 2,000 years ago, the enemies of Israel attempted to overthrow and erase God's covenantal relationship with Israel and the Jewish people. In two wars between the Jews and Rome in A.D. 70 and 135, the Romans destroyed the temple of God, exiled most of the Jewish people from the land of Israel, and changed Israel's name to Palestine. 226

227  Today, there are two competing names for the land of the Bible — Israel and Palestine. The name Israel reflects the will of God, and the name Palestine reflects the will of man. It was Satan's attempt to make the Word of God a lie and null and void.

Twenty-five hundred years ago, the prophet Ezekiel spoke of the restoration of the people of Israel to their land in the last days. Ezekiel spoke of dry bones coming to life and the Lord raising up His people, Israel, out of their graves and restoring them to their nation as an 228

exceedingly great army. Never before in history has a nation been destroyed and scattered all over the world, and then been brought back to life. It is a miracle and a fulfillment of Bible prophecy.

We read in Ezekiel 37:11–12, "Then he said to me: 'Son of man, these bones are the whole house of Israel. They say, "Our bones are dried up and our hope is gone; we are cut off." Therefore prophesy and say to them, "This is what the Sovereign Lord says: O my people, I am going to open your graves and bring you up from them; I will bring you back to the land of Israel. Then you, My people, will know that I am the LORD, when I open your graves and bring you up from them. I will put my Spirit in you and you will live, and I will settle you in your own land. Then you will know that I the LORD have spoken, and I have done it, declares the LORD" ' " (Ezek. 37:11–14).

Many believe these prophecies were fulfilled after World War II and the Holocaust, when Israel became a modern state, against all odds. Consider the utter devastation of the Jewish people, after one-third of the world's Jewish population was annihilated by the Nazis. Who could have imagined that they could ever be restored as a people and nation in their ancient homeland again?

At a time when the Jewish people were at one of their lowest ebbs in history, a miracle took place and God did raise them up, literally out of their graves, and made them into a nation once again.

Notice that the name of the land that the Lord will bring His people to in the last days is Israel, not Palestine.

229

Where did the name Palestine originate? The name Palestine was a regional name that was imposed on the area by the Roman emperor Hadrian who suppressed the second Jewish revolt in A.D. 135. He was so angry

with the Jews that he wanted to humiliate them and empha-
size that the Jewish nation had lost its right to a homeland
under Roman rule.

The name Palaestina was originally an adjective derived from Philistia, the archenemies of the Israelites 1,000
years earlier. Hadrian also changed the name of Jerusalem
to Aelia Capitolina, after his own family name, Aelia. He
forbade Jews from entering the city, except on the ninth
of the Hebrew month Av, to mourn the destruction of the
temple.

Since Hadrian was considered a god in the Roman Empire, this was his attempt to break God's covenant between
the Jewish people and their land. He effectively declared his
pagan authority over Jerusalem, which had been the place
of the presence of the God of Israel. To this day, the name
Palestine flies in the face of Israel and the entire issue can
be boiled down to a religious (spiritual) battle over a land
whose fate will be decided by the God of the Bible, since it
is His land (Lev. 25:23).

After 2,000 years of exile, who would have   **230**
thought that the Jewish people would one day
inhabit their land again and that it would be
called Israel? Certainly not the nations of the
world, who took turns occupying the land and
persecuting God's covenant people wherever
they could be found.

However, God had another plan when He
said, "I will bring back my exiled people Israel; they will
rebuild the ruined cities and live in them. They will plant
vineyards and drink their wine; they will make gardens
and eat their fruit. I will plant Israel in their own land,
never again to be uprooted from the land I have given
them" (Amos 9:14–15).

231

Yeshua (Jesus) also knew that Jerusalem would one day be overrun by Gentiles until just before His coming. In describing the signs of the end of the age, He said, "Jerusalem will be trampled on by the Gentiles until the times of the Gentiles are fulfilled" (Luke 21:24).

From the time of Hadrian until 1967, Jerusalem was controlled by Gentiles. It is now back in the hands of the Jewish people, which is one sign that the Messiah is soon to come to Zion.

God never forgot His people or His plan 232 for world redemption. On the one hand, His prophets spoke of the exile of the people and the deterioration of the land of milk and honey to a land of barrenness at the hands of the enemies of Israel (Ezek. 36:1–7). On the other hand, in His mercy, God also spoke of a prophetic day when His people, Israel, would be brought back from the four corners of the earth (Isa. 11:11–12), re-inhabit their land which would become fruitful again, and find complete spiritual renewal (Ezek. 36). We are seeing all of this happening today.

233

This prophetic process to restore the land and the people started just over 100 years ago, and is progressing at full force during our lifetime. God is preparing His land and His people for the soon coming of the Messiah. The Bible is full of prophetic Scriptures that we are seeing fulfilled before our eyes. The land of Israel and her people were not just tools of God to be used in days gone by and subsequently discarded. They were, and are, part of God's plan for the redemption of the world along with His church today. His mercies do endure forever.

In our day, instead of persecuting the Jewish people, millions of Bible-believing Christians are praying for the peace of Jerusalem and standing in support of God's prophetic plan.

The keeping of God's covenant promises to Israel today should be exciting news for the Church. Why? Because if God is faithful to His promises to Israel, then He will be faithful to His promises to the Church. As we await the coming of the Messiah, may we find ourselves to be part of His plan that will bring blessing to the whole world.

234

235

Most of the prophets who wrote the prophecies concerning the return of the Jewish people to their ancient homeland, Israel, lived in a day when the Jewish people were living in Israel and the land was inhabited and cultivated. Therefore, their predictions are even more amazing, because they accurately depicted the situation 2,500 years into the future. God was surely speaking His Word through them.

God said He would re-establish the nation of Israel in a day. Isaiah, the prophet, spoke of the re-creation of the nation of Israel at the end of the days before the Messiah comes. He said, "Who has ever heard of such a thing? Who has even seen such things? Can a country be born in a day or a nation be brought forth in a moment? Yet no sooner is Zion in labour than she gives birth to her children. . . . Rejoice with Jerusalem and be glad for her, all you who love her; rejoice greatly with her, all you who mourn over her" (Isa. 66:8–10).

236

237  On May 14, 1948, the modern state of Israel was born in a day! Interestingly, this occurred 50 years after the First Zionist Congress, held in 1897, where Theodore Herzl shared his vision of a Jewish state in Palestine, which he said would occur in 50 years time.

Ezekiel also saw that Israel would rise up as an exceedingly great army. Interestingly, the defense magazine *Jane's Weekly* has rated Israel as the fourth most efficient army in the world. One of the tiniest nations with one of the smallest populations in the world has one of the most powerful armies with which to defend themselves. In September 1999 it was reported that when the Israeli and U.S. military pilots staged mock dogfights in Israel, the Israelis had a score of 40:1 in one of the exercises. Yes, God has returned and strengthened His people.

238

David Ben-Gurion announces the establishment of the state of Israel on May 14, 1948.

239 Before the Children of Israel even entered into the Promised Land for the first time, Moses promised that God would bring them back to this land at times when they would be exiled from the land in judgment: "Then the LORD your God will restore your fortunes and have compassion on you and gather you again from all the nations where he scattered you. Even if you have been banished to the most distant land under the heavens, from there the LORD your God will gather you and bring you back. He will bring you to the land that belonged to your fathers, and you will take possession of it. He will make you more prosperous and numerous than your fathers" (Deut. 30:3–5).

240 Isaiah predicted that God's covenant people, the Jews, would return to Israel from the four corners of the earth. "In that day the Lord will reach out his hand a second time to reclaim the remnant that is left of his people from Assyria, from lower Egypt, from Upper Egypt, from Cush, from Elam, from Babylonia, from Hamath and from the islands of the sea. He will raise a banner for the nations and gather the exiles of Israel; he will assemble the scattered people of Judah from the four quarters of the earth" (Isa. 11:11–12).

Just over 100 years ago, the population of Palestine was sparse. But in the 1880s, Jews began to return — first, from Yemen, then from Czarist Russia to flee the pogroms. A trickle of Jewish immigrants became a steady stream. Today, Israel's population is over 6 million people, of which 80 percent are Jewish. They have now come from over 100 nations, and they continue to flood into their ancient homeland year after year.

241   Many Jews have come on their own because of their desire to live as Jews in their ancient, biblical homeland. For example, the Yemenite Jews who came in the 1880s declared that God spoke to them and told them it was time to go back to their ancient, biblical homeland. So, they packed their camels and walked across the Arabian desert to Jerusalem. Others have come because they were exiled from their homes, such as those who came in the early 1950s, having been expelled from Muslim countries. Still others have come due to extreme economic and social disruptions, such as we have seen in the countries of the former Soviet Union since 1989. There, as the economies of the CIS (Commonwealth of Independent States) continue to deteriorate and Jews are increasingly blamed for the troubles, they immigrate to Israel for a better life and a future in relative safety. Praise God that there is

Jewish Hagana ships transported Jewish refugees to Palestine even before Israel's statehood was declared.

an Israel for them to come to. Had there been an Israel in the 1930s, think of how many Jews would have been spared the horrors of the Nazi Holocaust.

Yes, Israel is a homeland open to all Jews from around the world who need a place to live and start a new life.

Isaiah predicted that the Jewish people would be specifically called out from the north and the south, and their return from the lands of the north would be even greater than the exodus from Egypt with Moses: "Do not be afraid, for I am with you; I will bring your children from the east and gather you from the west. I will say to the north, 'Give them up!' and to the south, 'Do not hold them back.' Bring my sons from afar and my daughters from the ends of the earth" (Isa. 43:5–6). Up until May 1991, this seemed like yet another unfulfilled prophetic passage concerning the return of the Jewish people to their ancient homeland. It seemed almost poetic until it was fulfilled specifically, to the word, as it was written.

242

For the past 100-plus years, Jews have been free to immigrate to Israel from the lands of the east and the west, with very little hindrance. However, the Jews of Eastern Europe and the former Soviet Union, as well as those in Ethiopia, were prevented from immigrating by Communist and Marxist governments. For decades, calls to "let my people go" from these lands were heard by Jews and Christians who demonstrated, and governments and social agencies who petitioned. Nevertheless, the Iron Curtain was closed tightly and only a few thousand were allowed to immigrate to Israel, while millions wanted to go.

Then, just as Isaiah predicted, the Iron Curtain lifted. With the breakup of the former Soviet Union, Jews were allowed to leave by the tens of thousands per month at its peak. Meanwhile, the Marxist Ethiopian government said in 1990 that the Ethiopian Jews could immigrate to Israel. They left their mountain villages on the Gondar region and made their way to the main airport in Addis Ababa. However, once there, the Ethiopian government held them back. They refused to go home and they camped out on the land around the airport for over one year. The Marxist government was then overthrown and, in a day, the U.S. CIA contacted U.S. President George Bush, who contacted Israeli Prime Minister Yitzhak Shamir. Over 35 planes were sent from Israel, in every conceivable shape and size, in an airlift called Operation Solomon. Nearly 15,000 Ethiopian Jewish immigrants were airlifted in a day. This is the first time that black Africans were taken from Africa out of bondage into freedom. When they arrived in Israel, they were all bused to the Western Wall plaza where they raised their hands to thank God for delivering them and bringing them home.

Consider that the prophet foresaw that the Jews of the north and the south would be prevented from coming to Israel, so that God himself would have to speak to these

Jewish immigrants arriving in Israel from the former Soviet Union.

nations. Note the specific words that God spoke. To the north, He said, "Give them up," and to the south, "Hold not back." The events show that the land of the north gave them up in large numbers. But, the land to the south held them back against their will. In a day, when the Ethiopian Marxist government was overthrown, the Jews were no longer held back. How specific and accurate are the words of God through His prophets.

243   Until this day, Jews continue to come to Israel from the lands to the north in a huge immigration of tens of thousands each year, over 1,000,000 people since 1989.

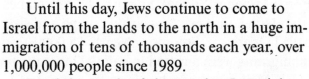

Read the words of the prophet Jeremiah, who saw the magnitude of this future immigration which is happening now and could still bring yet another 2,000,000 people, if time and money permit. Jeremiah wrote, " 'However, the days are coming,' declares the LORD, 'when men will no longer say, "As surely as the LORD lives, who brought the Israelites up out of Egypt," but they will say, "As surely as the LORD lives, who brought the Israelites up out of the land of the north and out of all the countries where he had banished them." For I will restore them to the land I gave to their forefathers. But now I will send for many fishermen,' declares the LORD, 'and they will catch them' " (Jer.16:14–16).

For 3,500 years, the Jewish people and the world have celebrated and remembered the exodus of the Jews from the clutches of Pharaoh. Yet God says that His exodus of His people from the lands of the north, in a future day, will be so great that it will even overshadow the exodus from Egypt. Today, the world is a witness of this prophetic move of God and many

244

Christian organizations have partnered with the Jewish Agency to rescue those who want to come.

245

God has promised to restore His barren land, Israel, and make it fruitful, inhabited, rebuilt, and more prosperous than at any time in history. When the Jews began to return from the nations of the world at the end of the 19th century, the land was barren and sparsely inhabited.

In the 1860s, the author Mark Twain traveled in what was then a backward region of the Ottoman Turkish Empire called Palestine, and described the land, thusly: "Nowhere in all the waste around was there a foot of shade." He called the land a "blistering, naked, treeless land." Of the Galilee, he said, "There is no dew, nor flowers, nor birds, nor trees.

Mark Twain

There is a plain and an unshaded lake, and beyond them some barren mountains." His summary of Palestine: "Of all the lands there are for dismal scenery, I think Palestine must be the prince. The hills are barren, they are dull of color, they are unpicturesque in shape. It is a hopeless, dreary, heartbroken land."[1] Yet, it was not God's will for His Land to remain in this condition.

246

Ezekiel's prophetic description of the "desolate ruins" of Israel (Ezek. 36:1–7) indicated that Israel became that way when the Jewish people were exiled from their land. Those who followed did not care for the land and it became barren. God chose this land for His people, Israel (Lev. 23:5–6), and neither the people nor the land prospered apart from one another.

However, Ezekiel goes on to say that a change was coming: "But you, O mountains of Israel, will produce branches and fruit for my people Israel, for they will soon come home. I am concerned for you and will look on you with favour; you will be ploughed and sown, and I will multiply the number of people upon you, even the whole house of Israel. The towns will be inhabited and the ruins rebuilt. I will increase the number of men and animals upon you, and they will be fruitful and become numerous. I will settle people on you as in the past and will make you prosper more than before. Then, you will know that I am the LORD. I will cause people, my people Israel, to walk upon you. They will possess you, and you will be their inheritance; you will never again deprive them of their children" (Ezek. 36:8–12).

Truly, the return of the Jews from over 100 nations of the world is a modern-day miracle. Yet they return to a horribly depleted land, as described by Mark Twain. Nevertheless, Ezekiel told us that the return of God's people would trigger the beginning of the restoration of the land, increase the fruitfulness of the land, the animals in the land, and the people on the land.

Isaiah says, "The desert and the parched **247** land will be glad; the wilderness will rejoice and blossom" (Isa. 35:1). Since those early days of the return of the Jews, the deserts have been reforested. Over 250 million trees have been planted by hand, with millions more germinating naturally from the seeds. The rocky fields are now fertile, the swamps are drained and planted, the ancient terraces have been rebuilt, and the ruined cities of old have been re-established.

248  Today, the barren deserts are truly and literally blossoming as a rose. In the Jordan Valley and the Negev Desert during the winter, farmers are producing and exporting over 5 million flowers a day. In fact, annually, Israel exports 1.5 billion flowers. Many of the flowers in the beautiful Amsterdam flower market are imported from Israel, and even re-exported to Arab and Muslim lands. In addition to flowers, fruit and vegetables are grown in the desert. Some, like melons, cucumbers, and tomatoes, are grown with underground brackish water to supply food year around to the tables of Israel and other nations. Special strains of apples and peaches have been developed to grow in the hot, dry desert climate of Israel, and now these varieties are grown in other parts of the world. Israel can grow apples and oranges in the same field (unheard of anywhere else in the world), and this tiny land offers tropical bananas and pineapples along with colder climate strawberries. Annually, over 150,000 tons of fruits and vegetables are exported from Israel, over and above feeding her own population.

In Israel today, fresh and saltwater ponds are providing the largest varieties of domestically produced fish in the world. These are being consumed in Israel and are also exported. The desert is fruitful and blossoming again, just as the prophets foretold.

The restoration, reforestation, and cultivation of the land has increased the vegetation and also changed the climate.

249

Israel is now a nation of over six million people that is a food-exporting nation. She boasts high levels of literacy, health, education and welfare, high technology, and agricultural development.

A desert region is now productive farmland.

In Israel, there is even a major restoration project, the Hai Bar Nature Project, aimed at restoring to Israel the animals mentioned in the Bible. So far, herds of oryx, Persian fallow deer, onager, roe deer, and other animals have been reintroduced to the land of Israel, having been hunted to extinction in centuries past.

An addax at the Hai Bar Nature Reserve.

The Bible said that there would be a prophetic day when God's people would even cherish the dust of Israel, signaling the time to favor Zion.

250

Speaking of God's restoration of Zion, the Psalmist says, "You will arise and have compassion on Zion, for it is time to show favour to her; the appointed time has come. For her stones are dear to your servants; her very dust moves them to pity. The nations will fear the name of the LORD, all the kings of the earth will revere your glory. For the LORD will rebuild Zion and appear in his glory" (Ps. 102:13–16).

While modern archaeology got its start in the last century, the exploration of the biblical land of Israel has seen its greatest efforts since the return of the Jewish people. The prophets speak of the ancient cities being rebuilt.

In this century, Jewish archaeologists have located thousands of ancient sites connected with Israel's historical, biblical past. All have been carefully preserved until there is time and money to excavate them. Meanwhile, the most important biblical cities have been excavated, and nearby, modern towns have been built with the same name as that of the ancient biblical site — just as the prophets foretold.

251 All around Israel, a road or a house cannot be built if the construction crews accidentally stumble upon buried history. Highways have been diverted and new buildings relocated so as to avoid damaging Israel's past.

It is said in Israel that every Israeli is an archaeologist. While this is not so professionally, it is certainly true that almost every Israeli knows something about archaeology and all seem to be amateur archaeologists. They truly "take pleasure in her stones and favor the dust," for every discovery reveals more of their past in this land. They painstakingly remove the dust from the stones at the archaeological sites, using small brushes so as not to disturb precious finds.

Today, the city of Jerusalem is like a large
archaeological garden, for all the finds have
been preserved for everyone to see, enjoy, and
learn about her history. Jerusalem has grown
in size and population greater than at any time
in her history. Psalm 102 confirms that when
the people of Israel love the stones and dust of
the land, and God builds up Zion, then He will
appear in Jerusalem in His glory. Considering this passage
along with the other fulfilled prophecies, it will not be long
until we see the Lord himself coming to Jerusalem.

252

253 God will change the heart of His people,
Israel, from stone to flesh.

The prophet Ezekiel speaks of a great end-
time miracle, which I call the three "Rs" of
prophecy concerning Israel. First, there is the
Return of the people to Zion. Second, there is
the Restoration of the land. And, third, there
is the Redemption of the heart of His people,
Israel. Let's see what God says: "For I will take you out
of the nations; I will gather you from all the countries and
bring you back into your own land. I will sprinkle clean water on you, and you will be clean; I will cleanse you from all
your impurities and from all your idols. I will give you a new
heart and put a new spirit in you; I will remove from you
your heart of stone and give you a heart of flesh. And I will
put my Spirit in you and move you to follow my decrees and
be careful to keep my laws. You will live in the land I gave
your forefathers; you will be my people, and I will be your
God" (Ezek. 36:24–28).

God chose the land of Israel for His people, Israel.
God makes it clear that the reconnection of the land and
the people in Israel is a key to the prosperity of both, both
physically and spiritually.

*Archaeological parks along the southern wall
of the Old City of Jerusalem*

We can see with our own eyes the prosperity and development of the land. While the people of Israel are far from perfect, there is a definite drawing to God in the hearts of those who come to Israel. The rhythm of the land is biblical; the national holidays are biblical; public buildings and parks are adorned with Scripture verses; the Bible is read at most official government events; Shabbat (Sabbath) is observed; and the Bible is discussed openly all over the country. After all, it is the Bible that describes the fact that both the land and the people exist because of the plans and purposes of God. Without Him, neither can fulfill their fullest purposes for the redemption of the world.

Are all in Israel closely following the Bible? No. Nevertheless, consider the hundreds of thousands of Jews who have come from former Communist lands who never saw a Bible or heard about God. Through no fault of their own, their hearts were as stone toward God. Now, in the land of Israel, they can read the Bible, hear about God, and worship Him openly — many for the first time in their lives. Just as the prophesy says, their hearts are becoming "as flesh" and warm toward God. Truly, God is drawing His people back to Him, as they are finding Him anew in His Holy Land.

God said He would use the non-Jews to **254** bless His nation and people, Israel. The prophet Isaiah says about Israel: "Arise, shine, for your light has come, and the glory of the LORD rises upon you" (Isa. 60:1). He goes on, "Surely the islands look to me; in the lead are the ships of Tarshish, bringing your sons from afar, with their silver and gold, to the honour of the LORD your God. . . . Foreigners will rebuild your walls, and their kings will serve you. . . . Your gates will always stand open, they will never be shut, day or night, so that men may bring you the wealth of the nations. . . . For the nation or kingdom that will not serve you will perish; it will be utterly ruined" (Isa. 60:9–12).

"This is what the Sovereign LORD says: 'See, I will beckon to the Gentiles, I will lift up my banner to the peoples; they will bring your sons in their arms and carry your daughters on their shoulders" (Isa. 49:22).

Paul teaches Christians that they have a debt to pay to the Jewish people, by blessing them in tangible ways (Rom. 15:27), as they too are grafted into the olive tree and share a covenant with the Jewish people. Christians today are helping to bring in the people of Israel, as well as bless the nation with their material contributions.

255   God desires to show the nations that He keeps His promises. Again, Ezekiel 36 declares that God is restoring His land and people to show the nations of the world that He is a faithful God who keeps His promises and His Word: "The desolate land will be cultivated instead of lying desolate in the sight of all who pass through it. They will say, 'This land that was laid waste has become like the garden of Eden; the cities that were lying in ruins, desolate and destroyed, are now fortified and inhabited.' Then the nations around you that remain will know that I the LORD have rebuilt what was destroyed and replanted what was desolate. I, the LORD, have spoken it, and I will do it" (Ezek. 36:34–36).

God is a god who cannot lie. He is a God about whom Jeremiah says, "Great is your faithfulness" (Lam. 3:23). Once He has spoken, He will fulfill His Word, which is part of the reason why He has moved heaven and earth to bring His land and people, Israel, back together in these days.   256

In a world that mostly disregards the Bible and the things of God, He is showing His faithfulness through Israel today, just as Ezekiel tells us. The nations can see the evidence of God's prophetic Word being fulfilled. Interestingly, this has been and is a catalyst for many to see the truth of God's Word and come to the Lord. The Church and even the Jewish people have had renewal and growth since the founding of the state of Israel. Fulfilled prophecy seen in so many areas brings God out of the realm of mere philosophy and back into the reality of daily life. He is a living God who chooses to interact with man. Just as in the days of the Bible, God is again interacting in a physical way with His people, Israel. While God does not need to be "proved," the fact that the world can "see" what He is doing today has brought many to faith.

257   Jesus taught that Jerusalem would be in the hands of Gentile nations until a time just before His coming. God promised to restore the worship of himself in the city of Jerusalem once again.

Luke 21:20–24 foresaw the destruction of Jerusalem and the exile of most of the people, which occurred in A.D. 70, with its final loss to the Jewish people in A.D. 135, both times at the hands of the Romans. From that time on, Jewish sovereignty of Jerusalem seemed to be only the stuff dreams are made of. Who would have ever thought Jerusalem would again be under Jewish sovereignty?

Well, many of the prophets of the Old Testament thought so, and so did Luke: "Jerusalem will be trampled on by the Gentiles until the times of the Gentiles are fulfilled" (Luke 21:24). Interestingly, in fulfillment of God's promises to Abraham, the redemptive Word of God went out to the nations for the purpose of converting the pagan

Gentiles into belief in the one God of Israel. However, this was only for a season, the "times of the Gentiles," at the end of which God would focus His attention again upon His people and land of Israel, and His city, Jerusalem.

In 1967, Luke's prophecy became a reality. The biblical portion of old Jerusalem, which had been in the hands of Gentile nations from A.D. 135 until 1967, was finally put back in the hands of the Jewish people. In June 1967, during the famous Six-Day War, the old city of Jerusalem once again fell into the hands of Israel — after about 1,900 years of exile. A picture of Israeli soldiers praying at the Western Wall attests to the sanctity of this moment in the life of Israel. The ancient holy city of Jerusalem was theirs again.

Would God now take this sacred old city away from Israel and give it to the Muslim world, which is what the Palestinian Authority and the Arab/Muslim world want? Interestingly, throughout most versions of the Bible, the word Palestine is never mentioned — only Israel and Jerusalem. Although the King James translators used the word "Palestine" in Joel 3:4, the biblical writers knew nothing of Palestine. The name was imposed by the Romans in the second century A.D., referencing Israel's ancient enemy, the Philistines. At the time of the King James translation, the Holy Land was still known as Palestine, hence the word usage in Joel. And, for us Christians, it is important to note that the

Bible records that Jesus is coming back to Jerusalem, not a Muslim city called El-Kuds, the name by which Jerusalem is called by the Muslim world.

Israeli soldiers at the Western Wall shortly after Jerusalem was liberated in June 1967.

There will be continued struggle over the **258**
city of Jerusalem until the second coming of the
Messiah (Christ), and the source of the battle
is spiritual. God is working to re-establish His
throne in Zion, and His enemies don't like it.
Nevertheless, God will prevail and the nations
will one day worship only Him in Jerusalem.

When the Jerusalem Council met (Acts
15) to decide on the degree of the law which had to be followed by the Gentiles who found faith in the God of Israel
through the Messiah Yeshua, James quoted from Amos
9:11–12. It is a description of the restoration of Jerusalem
to the worship of God, by Jews and Gentiles, at a future
time when the Messiah comes: " 'After this, I will return and
rebuild David's fallen tent. Its ruins I will rebuild, and I will
restore it, that the remnant of men may seek the Lord, and
all the Gentiles who bear my name, says the Lord, who does
these things' " (Acts: 15:16–17).

Interestingly, even the council members who lived in
Jerusalem where the Lord God of Israel was still being
worshiped understood the prophecy of Amos. It described
what would entail an exile and return of the Jewish people
to restore the worship of the God of the Bible, not pagan
gods, in the Holy City.

259  Zechariah foretells a time, after the Messiah comes, when "His feet will stand on the
Mount of Olives" (Zech. 14:4). "The Lord
will be king over the whole earth. On that day
there will be one Lord, and his name the only
name" (Zech. 14:9). "Then the survivors from
all the nations that have attacked Jerusalem
will go up year after year to worship the King,
the Lord Almighty, and to celebrate the Feast of Tabernacles" (Zech. 14:16).

While the worship of the God of Israel in His holy city Jerusalem has not reached its fullest measure, it is nevertheless moving toward this glorious day. Then there will be God's peace and presence in Jerusalem once again, and only He will be worshiped in His temple.

God will make Jerusalem the central focus of the world to judge the nations. The prophet Zechariah speaks boldly about God's use of Jerusalem at the end of days. He says, "I am going to make Jerusalem a cup that sends all the surrounding peoples reeling. Judah will be besieged as well as Jerusalem. On that day, when all the nations of the earth are gathered against her, I will make Jerusalem an immovable rock for all the nations. All who try to move it will injure themselves" (Zech. 12:2–3). "On that day I will set out to destroy all the nations that attack Jerusalem" (Zech. 12:9).

260

Interestingly, "on that day," which is a prophetic marker to indicate a future day, God says He will use Jerusalem as a standard by which to judge the nations of the world. Just as God has always used the land and the people of Israel to show the nations His glory, He is doing it again. Individually, our relationship to God is based on our salvation experience and our return to the Lord.

Nationally and politically, however, God can test the pulse of a nation by its attitude toward what He is doing in the land of Israel and the city of Jerusalem. This is God's litmus test: Do you understand My redemptive plan for the earth and support My will for Jerusalem to be restored to My people Israel in preparation for My soon arrival, or will you fight against it?

God promised that those who fight against His will for Jerusalem will incur the very wrath of God himself. They will be "cut in pieces" (Zech. 12:3;KJV). Now, it does not say that this will happen to all the nations of the earth. Rather, it says this destruction will happen to those nations who rise up against God's plans for Jerusalem. There is a national choice.

261   The stranger (those outside the covenant) will live among Israel and be treated with respect. "They [God's covenant people] will rebuild the ancient ruins and restore the places long devastated; they will renew the ruined cities that have been devastated for generations. Aliens will shepherd your flocks; foreigners will work your fields and vineyards" (Isa. 61:4–5). "If you [Israel] really change your ways and your actions and deal with each other justly, if you do not oppress the alien, the fatherless or the widow and do not shed innocent blood in this place, and if you do not follow other gods to your own harm, then I will let you live in this place, in the land I gave to your forefathers for ever and ever" (Jer. 7:5–7).

The "alien" or "foreigner" in these verses would include the Palestinian Arabs and other non-Jewish people who live in the land. They would receive a blessing by living and working in the land of Israel, not the land of Palestine. On the one hand, Israel should treat them with respect. On the other hand, they have the responsibility to live at peace, abiding by the laws of the land, recognizing under whose sovereignty it belongs.

This is what Moses taught: "The community [of Israel] is to have the same rules for you and for the alien living among you; this is a lasting ordinance for the generations to come. You and the alien shall be the same before the LORD: The same laws and regulations will apply both to you and to the alien living among you" (Num. 15:15–16).

When this relationship is broken, as has happened today, then crisis ensues.

The question for us today is this: If God is restoring Israel in preparation for the coming of the Messiah, is a Jewish Messiah coming to a divided Muslim city or a united Jewish city, where the God of Israel is being worshiped in His holy city? Those nations who seek to divide God's city again will be the nations who will come

262

up against Judah and Jerusalem to incur God's wrath. We have seen in recent years how the nations of the world have all ganged up on other nations who have been in error, e.g., Iraq, Haiti, Somalia, Serbia, etc. While this was necessary for these unruly nations, I believe the time will come when other nations will rise up against God's plans for Jerusalem and the Jewish people, because Israel is considered unruly.

For what reason, you may ask? The refusal of the Jews to allow Jerusalem to be divided again, and the holiest part given over to the Palestinian Authority as a Muslim capital of a Muslim state of Palestine. The nations believe this intransigence on the part of Israel to re-divide their city is an obstacle to the New World Order and their "god" of peace.

Which side of this argument will your nation take? Will you be for a partition of Jerusalem, or against it? Only through your prayers and speaking out to your government leaders can you work to keep your nation from being among those who come up against the continuation of a united Jerusalem under Jewish sovereignty. Please note, however, the Scripture is clear that if your nation supports a blockade of Jerusalem for the purpose of dividing the city again, it will be judged severely by God.

263

God's covenant people will return to their ancient homeland, never to be exiled from their land again.

Some critics of Israel say all of the prophecies described herein do not apply to Israel

today. Rather, they say all of these prophecies were fulfilled when the Jewish people returned from the Babylonian exile in the 6th century B.C. However, the fulfillment
of these passages in our day has been specific to these
verses, and the magnitude of the fulfillment has never occurred to this degree at any other time in history. Whatever degree of fulfillment took place when the Jews returned
from Babylon, it was only a small picture of a greater
fulfillment to come.

Nevertheless, Amos 9:14–15 proves that the Babylonian
exile and return is not what He was talking about, when
God says: " 'I will bring back my exiled people Israel; they
will rebuild the ruined cities and live in them. They will
plant vineyards and drink their wine; they will make gardens and eat their fruit. I will plant Israel in their own land,
never again to be uprooted from the land I have given them,'
says the LORD your God."

Note the last verse, when it says, "NEVER AGAIN to
be uprooted from the land I have given them." After the return from Babylon, the Jewish people were uprooted again,
so it is obvious that Amos was talking about yet another
exile and return, which I believe is fulfilled in the Roman
exiles and today's return!

In the New Testament, there are many
occasions when the author is referencing the
fulfillment of specific prophecies and uses
words like, "according to the Scripture" refer-
ring to a fulfilled prophecy in the Old Testament. When Jesus (Yeshua) was reading an
Isaiah prophecy in His home synagogue in
Nazareth, He concluded the messianic read-
ing by saying, "This day is this Scripture fulfilled in your
ears" (Luke 4:21; KJV). The "this-is-that" declaration of
a fulfilled prophecy is powerful, because we are able to see

264

that God does fulfill His Word, and it brings faith to the heart of man.

This book is not attempting to speculate on the future as through a crystal ball. Rather, I have used the "this-is-that" method of interpretation to show that so many of the prophetic passages of the Bible have been fulfilled in our lifetime — to the letter. For me, and for many others, seeing God at work in this day is a real faith booster.

265   Let us move our faith out of the realm of mere philosophy and religious duty into a dynamic walk with the living God of Israel who is not only fulfilling His miracles for His people Israel, but for His church. We need to realize that the time is short before the coming of the Messiah, and therefore we must work double-time to bring God's redemptive message found in the Bible to a hurting world in great spiritual need of God's truth.

The day of Israel's full restoration is near. The Messiah will make it possible and we shall all live in peace. Until He comes, we, who believe the Bible to be God's Word and that every promise of God will come to pass, must stand and support Israel's right to its land. It is a divine right. We must be patient with those who do not believe the Bible, nor accept Israel's right to the land, yet with love for all, we must strongly support Israel's right. We cannot do otherwise and have a clear conscience. We cannot say on the one hand that we believe there is a God who has revealed His perfect will in His Holy Scriptures, and on the other hand deny Israel its right to the land God promised to her.

266

267

Our commitment to Israel was penned by the Psalmist so long ago: "You will arise and have compassion on Zion, for it is time to show favour to her; the appointed time has come" (Ps. 102:13). Again the Psalmist exhorts us: "Pray for the peace of Jerusalem: 'May those who love you be secure. May there be peace within your walls and security within your citadels.' For the sake of my brothers and my friends, I will say, 'Peace be within you.' For the sake of the house of the LORD our God, I will seek your prosperity" (Ps. 122:6–9).

CHAPTER SIX

HISTORY
AND ISRAEL TODAY

The Jewish people have had an inseparable   268
relationship with the land of Israel, the land
of the Bible, for the past 4,000 years, since the
days of Abraham. There have been ebbs and
flows in Jewish habitation of the land, yet at no
time were the Jewish people totally absent from
the land.

While their exile under the Assyrians and
Babylonians was relatively short-lived, the last, greater exile
by the Romans lasted almost 1,800 years. But God said He
would restore His people, Israel, to their land in one final
and great return and restoration.

As we have seen elsewhere in this book, there are a mul-
titude of biblical prophecies concerning the regathering of
the Jewish people from around the world to a barren land
that would be restored to its former glory. This began to
unfold in the late 1800s.

Events leading to the establishment of the modern state
of Israel began during the period when the Ottoman (Turkish) Empire controlled the region, then called Palestine.

269

The chronology of past invaders who ruled
in the land of Israel reads like a "Who's Who of
World Empires." The land of Israel was a choice
fruit that everyone wanted to pluck for their
own ends. The strategic location and characteristics that made this land desirable enough to be
chosen by the Lord as "His Land" also made it

the focus of empires who wanted to rule the world. In some cases, they just wanted to overrule the Jewish people because they were the people of God, and some of these world powers were opposed to the things of God. Israel and the Jewish people are some of those important "things" of God.

According to many scholars, the patriarchs 270 Abraham, Isaac, and Jacob were active in Canaan between 2100 and 1875 B.C. The birthright to the covenant established with Abraham in Genesis 12:1–3 was passed on from Abraham to Isaac (not Ishmael or the other sons of Abraham), to Jacob (not Esau), and through Jacob's 12 sons who became known as the Twelve Tribes of Israel.

271 The 12 sons of Jacob were Reuben, Simeon, Levi, Judah, Zebulun, Issachar, Dan, Gad, Asher, Napthtali, Joseph, and Benjamin. God withdrew Levi from the list of tribes in order to use the Levites in the transport and care of the tabernacle and its service (Num. 1:47–53). Why Joseph was withdrawn from the list we are not told, but his two sons, Ephraim and Manasseh (two half-tribes), were selected to make up the number of 12. Some suggest it was an expression of the double portion of inheritance to a first-born son, showing that Joseph's dream was, in fact, true, even though he was not the first-born.[1]

After Jacob's son Joseph was sold into slav- 272 ery and eventually became the prime minister of Egypt, the rest of the family found refuge there from a regional famine. They remained in Egypt, and the Hebrews ultimately became slaves under a pharaoh "that knew not Joseph."

273

As promised, about 400 years after Joseph first came to Egypt, a redeemer was raised up to bring the Children of Israel out of the land of Egypt in a great Exodus. His name was Moses. It was God's intention for the Children of Israel to move into the Promised Land directly, but they chose to stay in the desert after receiving the report from the 12 spies that the people of the land were powerful and that their cities were heavily fortified. Despite the fact that Joshua and Caleb brought examples of the produce of the land — grapes, figs, and pomegranates — the people chose not to enter. Not violating their free will, God kept them in the desert for 40 years, so that the second generation was the one to move into and conquer the Promised Land.

Even though the first generation of Hebrews who left Egypt in the Exodus showed a lack of faith in God by choosing not to enter the Promised Land immediately, God was still with them. He provided shelter, food (manna and quail), shoes that would not wear out, and showed himself in a pillar of cloud by day and a pillar of fire by night. He still loved them even though they disobeyed Him. He protected them so that their children could fulfill His calling to enter into His land. That should be a warning to us. Even though God may be with us, have we taken the necessary risks to fulfill our calling, our "promised land" in life?

274

275

After God brought Joshua and the Israelites into the Promised Land, it took hundreds of years to conquer the land, just as God had said: "The LORD your God will drive out those nations before you, little by little. You will not

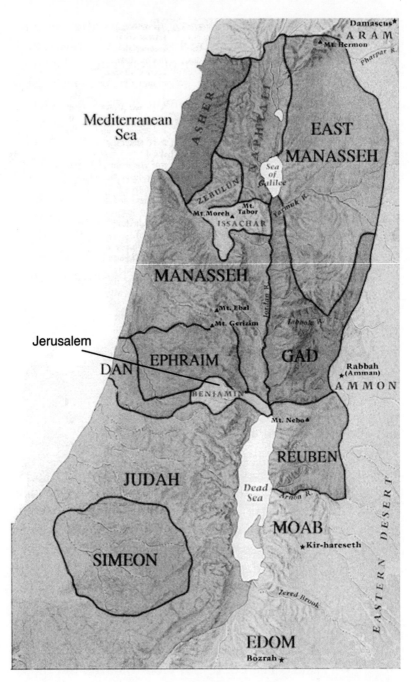

Map 7

be allowed to eliminate them all at once, or the wild animals will multiply around you. But the LORD your God will deliver them over to you, throwing them into great confusion until they are destroyed. He will give their kings into your hand, and you will wipe out their names from under heaven. No one will be able to stand up against you; you will destroy them. The images of their gods you are to burn in the fire" (Deut. 7:22–25).

The Bible is very specific as to where the Twelve Tribes of Israel were settled in the land, describing their territorial claims in great detail (Josh 15–19). With a Bible and a current map of Israel, you can still trace the borders of these tribal regions (see map 7). 276

Reuben, Gad, and the half-tribe of Manasseh were settled on the east side of the Jordan River (Num. 32:33). The other 9-1/2 tribes were settled west of the Jordan.

277 Saul became Israel's first king about 1050 B.C. However, it was only under Kings David and Solomon, Israel's second and third kings, that the nation fully consolidated into the Davidic (1010–970 B.C.) and Solomonic (970–930 B.C.) empires. Solomon's empire incorporated all the land from the Sinai Desert up to the Euphrates River, but not the totality of what God had promised to Israel. Prophetically, this will come to pass in a future day. 278

In 1004 B.C., Jerusalem became the capital of a United Israel, by God's choice. It was specially located to be the administrative and spiritual center of the kingdom, on the border between the tribal areas of Judah and Benjamin. It was not located on any major trade route, nor a major waterway or seaport, or near an economic or agricultural resource. Jerusalem's only main attraction was the Temple of the Lord and His presence, even in the past. Other empires and religions only wanted to conquer Jerusalem because of its spiritual identity and importance in the Bible.

279

David conquered the city and bought the threshing floor of Araunah for 50 shekels of silver for the house of the Lord. Eventually Solomon built the temple (2 Chron. 3:1), and to this day, the only recorded legal deed for this land is in the Bible, and it clearly belongs to the Jewish people. However, instead of there being a Jewish temple to the Lord there today, there are several Muslim mosques on this site and religious Jews and Christians are forbidden to pray on the Temple Mount. Yet, according to the Bible and history, it is a sacred area that does not belong to the Muslims, but to the Jews. It is also the site for the third temple that is yet to be built (Ezek. 40–44), so one day its status will change.

280

After Solomon's death in 930 B.C., the United Kingdom was divided into a northern kingdom (Israel), with its capital in Samaria, and a southern kingdom (Judah), with its capital in Jerusalem.

281

The major kings of the northern kingdom (Israel) were Jeroboam I (928–907 B.C.), Nadah (907–906), Baasha (906–883), Omri (882–871), Ahab (871–852), Joram (852–842), Hehu (842–814), Jehoahaz (814–800), Jehoash (800–784), Jeroboam II (784–748),

Menahem (747–737), Pekahiah (737–735), Pekah (735–733), and Hoshea (733–724). The line ended with the Assyrian captivity in 722 B.C.

The major kings of the southern kingdom (Judah) were Rehoboam (928–911 B.C.), Abijah (911–908), Asa (908–867), Jehoshaphat (867–846), Jehoram (846–843), Athaliah (842–836), Joash (836–798), Amaziah (798–769), Uzziah (769–733), Jotham (750–735), Ahaz (733–727), Hezekiah (727–698), Manasseh (698–642), Josiah (639–609), Jehoiakim (608–598), and Zedekiah (596–586). The line ended with the Babylonian captivity in 586 B.C.[2]

The major prophets of the northern kingdom (Israel) were Elijah (875–848 B.C.), Elisha (848–797), Jonah (785–775), Amos (760–750), and Hosea (750–715).

282

The major prophets of the southern kingdom (Judah) were Obadiah (855–c. 840), Isaiah (740–681), Jeremiah (626–585), and Ezekiel (593–571). After the exile, we find Daniel (605–530), Zechariah (520–480), and Malachi (440–430).[3]

283

In 722 B.C., judgment came upon the northern kingdom when Sennacherib, king of Assyria, conquered it, but unsuccessfully laid siege to Jerusalem. King Hezekiah built an underground water tunnel that emptied into the Pool of Siloam, so that the people had water inside the city walls. The angel of God killed Sennacherib's army on the hills around Jerusalem and he went home in shame (2 Kings 19).

In the stele record of his life that is found in the museum, Sennacherib recorded the event just as it is told in the Bible.

In 586 B.C., the southern kingdom of Judah eventually fell to Nebuchadnezzer, king of Babylon, who captured and destroyed Jerusalem, dismantling the first temple of God. The ark of the covenant disappeared at this time. Many speculate on where it is, but no one has made such a discovery public. Judah was taken into captivity in Babylon (2 Kings 25).

284

285

In 539–537 B.C., following a decree by the Persian king Cyrus, who had conquered Babylonia, some Jews returned to Israel. An estimated 50,000 embarked on their first return, led by Zerubbabel, a descendant of the house of David.[4] The first thing the people did was to re-establish the temple of the Lord, as recorded in the Book of Ezra. Less than a century later, in 445 B.C., a second return was led by Ezra the scribe and Nehemiah. They undertook a massive reconstruction and fortification of the city walls and the further development of the temple of the Lord, as recorded in the Book of Nehemiah. The establishment of this second temple was ultimately enlarged and beautified by Herod the Great, 500 years later.

The repatriation of the Jews, Ezra's inspired leadership, the building of the second temple, the refortification of Jerusalem's walls, and the establishment of the Knesset HaGedolah (Great Assembly), which was the supreme religious and judicial body of the Jewish people, marked the beginning of the Second Commonwealth (Second Temple Period). Within the confines of the Persian Empire, Judah was a nation centered in Jerusalem, whose leadership was no longer under a king, but entrusted to the high priest and the Council of Elders.[5]

286

Alexander the Great

287

In 350 B.C., the Persians captured Jerusalem. This was closely followed by the Greeks under the leadership of Alexander the Great, in 332 B.C. After Alexander died, the region was divided up among his three chief generals. In 313 B.C., Ptolemy I of Egypt ruled Jerusalem. Then, in 170 B.C., the Seleucid king, Antiochus Epiphanes IV, king of Syria, plundered Jerusalem and forced the Jews to stop worshiping the God of Israel and to worship the pagan gods of the Greeks. During this time, many Jews followed Greek customs and became Hellenized, while others resisted.

288

When Antiochus Epiphanes IV desecrated the temple by sacrificing a pig on the altar of God and forced the Jewish people in the towns and villages to do the same, this was too much for some religious Jews. In 167–164 B.C., the Hasmoneans revolted, led at first by Mattathias of the priestly Hasmonean family, and upon his death by his son Judas, known as the Maccabee (hammer). The terms Hasmoneans or Maccabeans can be used interchangeably.

On the 25th of Kislev, 165 B.C., the Hasmoneans captured the temple, which they purified for proper worship. However, they only had enough sacramental oil for the temple lamp stand for one day. Yet, God allowed it to burn for eight days, until enough new oil could be prepared. From this miracle, we get the holiday of Hannukah that is still celebrated today. Jesus also celebrated this holiday, which was also known as the Feast of Dedication, "Then came the Feast of Dedication. It was winter" (John 10:22).

The Hasmonean Empire was quite success- **289** ful and achieved independence from the Seleu- cids. The Hasmonean rulers became hereditary kings and regained boundaries not far short of Solomon's kingdom. During the period of the Hasmonean dynasty, which lasted about 80 years (142–63 B.C.), political consolidation under Jewish rule was attained and Jewish life flourished again in Israel and Jerusalem.

290 However, in 63 B.C., the Romans invaded the region, led by Pompeii. They granted the Hasmonean king, Hyrcanus II, limited author- ity under the Roman governor of Damascus. The Jews did not accept the Roman rule well, as evidenced by numerous insurrections. The last attempt to restore the former glory of the Has- monean dynasty was made by Mattathias Anti- gonus in 40 B.C. His defeat and death three years later at the hands of the Romans brought Hasmonean rule to an end, and the land became a vassal state of the Roman Empire.[6]

In 37 B.C., Herod, son of an advisor to **291** King Hyrcanus II and married to his daughter, was appointed king of Judea by the Romans. Although he had no authority in foreign policy, he was granted almost unlimited autonomy in the country's internal affairs, and became one of the most powerful monarchs in the eastern part of the Roman Empire.[7] The main regional names for the area can be found in the New Testament. They are Judea, Samaria, and Galilee, west of the Jordan

River, and the Decapolis and Perea, east of the Jordan River. Palestine is a name given to the land by the Romans 100 years after the death and resurrection of Jesus.

292   Herod was known as a master builder and built a huge port city in Caesarea (named after Caesar) and fortifications: the Herodian (southeast of Bethlehem), Sabastia in the mountains of Samaria, and Masada on the western shore of the Dead Sea.

Jerusalem, however, was Herod's crown jewel, where his building programs went on for decades as he made this city one of the wonders of the world. In 20 B.C., Herod began the expansion and beautification of the temple, which must have been a sight to behold from the Mount of Olives, as the pilgrims came from the Jordan Valley up to Jerusalem.

Herod's fortress, called the Herodian.

Jesus was born in approximately 3 B.C. and 293
spent His entire life and ministry in the land
of Israel. The religious and political influences
of this period greatly affected His ministry
and ultimately resulted in His crucifixion in
Jerusalem, which was then part of the Roman
province of Judea. His resurrection and the
subsequent spread of Christianity changed the
course of history.

294 Herod was not a very popular king for
mainly two reasons. He was a puppet of the
 Romans who were occupiers and made the
people subject to Rome. More importantly,
Herod was Idumean (from the line of Esau),
making him illegitimate as a true king of Israel
because he was from the wrong covenant/fami-
ly line. This was a clever choice for the Romans,
because Herod was acceptable enough to be king, but also
unacceptable enough that they knew the people would never
follow him into a revolt.

In A.D. 6, Judea was brought under direct 295
Roman administration, because the heirs of
Herod who sat on the throne of Judea became
progressively ineffective. Simultaneous with the
introduction of direct Roman rule, a Jewish re-
sistance movement, called the Zealots, began to
organize and rebel against Rome. Eventually, a
full-scale revolt against Roman rule took place
in A.D. 66–73. In A.D. 70, the Roman siege of Jerusalem
lasted for 134 days, resulting in the sacking of Jerusalem by
Titus and the destruction of the second temple of God.

According to the first century historian Flavius Josephus, an estimated one million Jews perished in the siege of

Masada

Jerusalem alone, with many killed elsewhere in the country and tens of thousands sold into slavery.

296   Nearly 1,000 Jewish men, women, and children who had survived the fall of Jerusalem occupied and fortified King Herod's mountaintop palace complex of Masada on the western shore of the Dead Sea. For three years they held out against repeated Roman attempts to dislodge them. When the Romans finally broke through the fortress, they found that the defenders and their families had chosen to die rather than be enslaved. Ten

men were chosen by lot to kill everyone, then one killed the nine and only one killed himself. The ten lots, written on broken pottery shards, were discovered by archaeologists when Masada was excavated in the 1960s and 1970s.

After the fall of Jerusalem, the Sanhedrin   297
(Supreme Jewish Council headed by the high priest with religious, civil, and criminal juris- diction) was reconvened in Yavneh and later in Tiberias. With the second temple (the central focus of Judaism) destroyed, the Sanhedrin needed to interpret how Judaism would be practiced. The priests of the temple were re- placed by community rabbis and, in the absence of a central place of worship, the synagogue became the hub of each Jewish community. Judaism had to be reinterpreted so that it could survive without the temple in Jerusalem.

298   Meanwhile, Christianity was spreading throughout the world. According to the Book of Acts, Jerusalem was the seat of the first Church Council (Acts 15) and remained the center of the faith for centuries. Christianity spread from Jerusalem out to the provinces of the Roman Empire, yet encountered opposi- tion, because new religions were forbidden under Roman law. Christianity was considered an illegal religion, and Christians were gravely persecuted and even put to death for their faith.

299

There was a brief period of Jewish sover- eignty at the turn of the first century, which was followed by a revolt of Shimon Bar Ko- chbah from A.D. 132–135. There was a large- scale slaughter of Jews. Jerusalem was razed

and then rebuilt by the Roman emperor Hadrian and re-named "Aelia Capitolina," after himself (his family name being Aelia). Jews were excluded from Jerusalem. To further blot out the connection between the Jews and the land of Judea, Samaria, and Galilee, Hadrian renamed it Syria Palestina, a name that remains in opposition to the name "Israel" to this day. The pagan world thought they had broken the covenants of God between the Jewish people and the land.

300   Constantine, the emperor of Rome, espoused Christianity in A.D. 306. No longer was Christianity persecuted in the Empire. Rather, it became the religion of the Empire and the Jewish people were persecuted. In A.D. 324, the Holy Roman army swept into Jerusalem to claim the origins of the faith and established Byzantine rule. In 326, Queen Helena (mother of Byzantine Emperor Constantine) visited Jerusalem and began building major churches including Holy Sepulchre in Jerusalem and the Church of the Nativity in Bethlehem.

Constantine

301    Early in the seventh century at the dawn of Islam, Jerusalem changed hands several times. In 614, the Byzantine Empire lost Jerusalem to the Persians, and then regained it in 629. However, in 638, Islamic forces swept in, under the Caliph Omar Ben Hatav, capturing Jerusalem

and the land of the Bible and placing it under Arab Muslim rule. From 688–691, the Dome of the Rock was built by Abdal-Malik on the Temple Mount. Even though it is the most prominent feature on the Temple Mount, the more holy site to the Muslims is the Al Aksa Mosque, which was a Byzantine church before being converted into a mosque. Supposedly, Mohammed stopped off at this site on his way to heaven, even though Jerusalem is never mentioned in the Koranic texts.

302

Life under Islamic rule continued uninterrupted for about 400 years, with caliphs ruling first from Damascus, then from Baghdad and Egypt. In the 11th century, conflict between Muslims and Christians began to increase. In 1009, the Muslim Caliph Hakim ordered the destruction of churches and synagogues.

303

In 1096, the first crusades from Europe captured Jerusalem. This crusader rule lasted until 1291. When the crusaders entered the land, they slaughtered Muslims and Jews in their wake. They even killed many Christians because they "looked" Middle Eastern and were assumed to be Muslims. In Jerusalem, Jews were found praying in their synagogues for God's mercy when found by the crusaders. By crusader accounts, they put wood around the synagogues and burned the Jews alive while they sang the hymn, "Christ, We Adore Thee." Those who were not killed were sold into slavery.

304

In 1099, the First Latin/Christian Kingdom was established by Godfrey of Bouillon. In 1187, the Muslim warrior Saladin captured

Jerusalem from the crusaders. In 1192, Richard the Lion-hearted tried and failed to reconquer Jerusalem. Yet the crusaders remained in the land until 1291 when Muslim Mameluks from Egypt put an end to crusader domination of the land, as they conquered the entire region. The crusaders mainly concentrated on fortifying cities and building castles. They also opened up transportation routes from Europe that allowed for better trade and an onslaught of Christian pilgrimage. Although the land was under Christian domination, it did not become a Christian country.

305   The Mameluks ruled from 1291–1516 and the land became a forgotten province ruled from Damascus. Akko, Jaffa, and other ports were destroyed for fear of new crusades, and international commerce was interrupted. The urban centers were virtually in ruins, most of Jerusalem was abandoned, and the small Jewish community living there was poverty-stricken. The period of Mameluk decline was darkened by political and economic upheavals, plagues, locust invasions, and devastating earthquakes.[8]

*The Golden or Eastern Gate, sealed by
the Muslims in 1541*

In 1517, Turkish Sultan Selim conquered   **306**
Jerusalem and the land of Israel for the Ottoman Empire. Turkish rule lasted until 1917,
when World War I resulted in the breakup
of this empire into multiple states within the
Middle East.

In 1535–1538, the Turkish Suleiman the
Magnificent rebuilt the ramparts and wall
around Jerusalem. In 1541, the Muslims sealed the Golden
Gate to prevent the Messiah's entrance (as according to
Jewish tradition).

The Ottoman Turks divided the land into four districts
and attached it administratively to Damascus.

307   At the beginning of Ottoman rule, it is

estimated that only 1,000 Jewish families lived
in the country, residing mainly in Jerusalem,
Nablus, Hebron, Gaza, Safed, and the villages
of Galilee. The community was comprised of
descendants of Jews who had never left the
land, as well as immigrants from North Africa
and Europe.

Under the Turks, Jews immigrated to the land, with as
many as 10,000 settling in Safed.

The 19th century saw signs of Western   **308**
progress, with European powers jockeying
for position, often through missionary activi-
ties. British, American, and French scholars
launched studies of biblical geography and
archaeology, consulates were opened in Jerusalem, steamships began to bring travelers
and trade from Europe, postal and telegraphic
connections were installed, and the first road was built
connecting Jerusalem and Jaffa. The land's rebirth as the

Yemin Moshe today

crossroads of three continents was accelerated by the open-
ing of the Suez Canal.[9]

309   Of all the groups living in Jerusalem, since
1818 the Jewish population has been the religious majority. The first official census in 1844
confirms Jewish religious majority — 7,120
Jews, 5,760 Muslims, and 3,390 Christians.
       Up until 1860, everyone in Jerusalem lived
inside the walls of the ancient city and the gates

were secured at sunset each day. At this time, the population had grown to the point that there was no more room.

The first Jewish suburb, Mishkenot Sha'ananim, was built near the Jaffa Gate outside the Old City walls in 1860 by Sir Moses Montefiore. Seven similar neighborhoods were also built outside the walls, that is, Nahlat Shiva (1869), Mea Shearim (1873–75), Yemin Moshe (1892), etc. These became the nucleus of the new city of Jerusalem. Some are the quaintest and most interesting neighborhoods of Jerusalem today. By 1880, the Jewish population was the absolute majority in Jerusalem.

In the 1880s, we begin to see major fulfillments of Bible prophecy concerning the Jewish people and the land of Israel.

310

The modern state of Israel is directly connected to biblical Israel, as attested to by its history and the manner in which its modern rebirth has so closely coincided with Bible prophecy.

Just as God arranged for Joshua to bring the Children of Israel into the Promised Land 3,500 years ago, in our day God arranged for the Jewish people to come back to their ancestral homeland!

311 The Turkish Ottoman Empire ruled the entire Middle East region from 1516–1917.

During this 400 years of harsh Turkish rule, the land of Palestine (Israel) was sparsely populated, mostly by nomadic peoples. By the end of the 18th century, much of the land was owned by absentee landlords and leased to impoverished tenant farmers.

The land was poorly cultivated and a widely neglected expanse of eroded hills, sandy deserts, and malarial marshes encroached on what was left of agricultural land. Its ancient irrigation systems, terraces, towns, and villages had crumbled.

Taxation was crippling, with even its few trees being taxed. When the people could not pay the tax, the trees were cut down to fuel the steam engines carrying goods between Istanbul, Beirut, Damascus, and Cairo. The great forests of the Galilee and the Carmel mountain range were denuded of trees; swamp and desert encroached on agricultural land. "Palestine" was truly a poor, neglected, no-man's land with no important cities.

Mark Twain, who visited Palestine in 1867, **312** described it as a "desolate country whose soil is rich enough, but is given over wholly to weeds — a silent mournful expanse. . . . We never saw a human being on the whole route. . . . There was hardly a tree or a shrub anywhere. Even the olive and the cactus, those fast friends of a worthless soil, had almost deserted the country."[10]

313   The report of the Palestine Royal Commission (British) quotes an account of the condition of the coastal plain along the Mediterranean Sea in 1913: "The road leading from Gaza to the north was only a summer track suitable for transport by camels and carts . . . no orange groves, orchards, or vineyards were to be seen until one reached Yavne village . . . houses were all of mud. Schools did not exist. . . . The western part, towards the sea was almost a desert. . . . The villages in this area were few and thinly populated . . . many villages were deserted by their inhabitants."

The French author Voltaire described Palestine as "a hopeless, dreary place." In short, under the Turks, the land suffered both from neglect and a low population. 314

Today, the land is rejoicing with life, which has been restored to the country since the Jewish people began their return in the late 1800s. This process has not been without its difficulties. Remember, however, when we read the Book of Joshua, we see that even though God said He was bringing the Israelites into their Promised Land, which He gave them, the movement into the land was not without its great problems. The enemies of the Bible and God's plans are always in opposition to it.

315 In the 1880s, while still under Turkish rule, it is as though a giant electro-magnet were turned on in the land of Israel. Jews began to immigrate to what was then called Palestine. They came from Yemen in the south, Russia in the north, Morocco in the west, and Iraq in the east. This move into Israel was the beginning of the fulfillment of the prophetic return to Zion, which has been taking place over the past 125 years in a series of *aliyot*, or large moves of Jewish populations into the land of Israel. (*Aliyah* is a Hebrew term for "going up to Zion" or immigration.)

Despite a myriad of difficulties, the Jewish people were not prevented from coming home to Zion by the millions. The first *aliyah* (immigration) started in the 1880s when new Jewish communities began to spring up, including Petah Tikva, Rosh Pinna, Rishon le Zion, Gedera, and Zichron Ya'acov. Jews purchased 316

land at high prices, 73 percent of it from the absentee Arab landlords who lived in Cairo, Damascus, and Beirut.

About 80 percent of the Arabs living in Palestine came from different parts of the Ottoman Empire to work for these landlords and were debt-ridden peasants, semi-nomads, and Bedouins.[11] Most of the land purchased had not been cultivated previously because it was swampy, rocky, sandy, or for some other reason regarded as undesirable for cultivation.

According to the Peel Commission (British, 1937): "The Arab charge that the Jews have obtained too large a proportion of good land cannot be maintained. Much of the land now carrying orange groves was sand dunes or swamp and uncultivated when it was purchased."

Moreover, the price the Jews paid for this barren land was exorbitant. In 1944, Jews paid between $1,000 and $1,100 per acre in Palestine, mostly for arid or semi-arid land. In the same year, rich black soil in Iowa was selling for about $110 per acre (U.S. Dept. of Agriculture).[12]

317   In 1897, Jewish leaders, moved by Theodore Herzl, formally organized the Zionist movement at the First Zionist Congress in Basle, Switzerland. They called for the restoration of the Jewish National Home in Palestine where Jews could have sanctuary, self-determination, and the renascence of their ancient civilization and culture.

Theodore Herzl

In 1898, Theodore Herzl met Kaiser Wilhelm just outside Jerusalem's Jaffa Gate.

William Hechler, a Bible-believing Protestant and Christian Zionist, had a profound influence on Herzl, as he supported and motivated him to continue with his goal of establishing a Jewish State in Palestine. Hechler was motivated by his reading of the Bible prophets and his belief that the God of Israel was able to fulfill these prophecies for His people, Israel, in their ancient homeland.

At the First Zionist Congress in 1897, Herzl predicted that in 50 years, the state of Israel would be a reality. Exactly 50 years later, in 1947, the United Nations voted for Israel to be a state (November 29, 1947), and on May 14, 1948, the new flag of Israel was raised.

318

319

Meanwhile, Jews began to come in waves from different parts of the world. What was called the "second aliyah," or the second wave of Jewish immigration, took place in the early 1900s. They came from Russia as a result of the pogroms against the Jewish citizens there. The movie *Fiddler on the Roof* depicts Jewish life in Russia at this time, when many were forced to leave. Some Jews came to Palestine.

As the Jews returned to their ancient homeland and began to develop the region, Arabs from many parts of the impoverished, decaying Ottoman Empire of the Middle East rushed into Palestine to get jobs. Most of today's "Palestinians" are descendants of these newcomers.

320

321   The Middle East became enveloped in World War I, which began in 1914. In 1916, even before Britain and France had conquered the Ottoman Empire, they set up an Anglo-French commission to submit an agreed plan for the postwar partition of the Ottoman Empire. The British representative was Sir Mark Sykes and the French representative was Charles Francois Georges-Picot. The agreement became known as the Tripartite (Sykes-Picot) Agreement of 1916, which effectively drew the borders of the new states of the Middle East. Their interests were more in favor of the strategic interests of Britain and France, not necessarily of the people who would live in this region. Consequently, Kurdistan was apportioned to Turkey, Syria, Iraq, and Iran, and to this day the Kurds are disenfranchised.

Most of the modern Arab states of the   322
Middle East owe their borders to the Sykes-Picot Agreement, as does Israel.

While many believe that Israel is a new state to the region, having only acquired its sovereignty in 1948, it needs to be remembered that the other Middle East states also acquired their independence in the 20th century, e.g., Saudi Arabia (1913), Lebanon (1920), Iraq (1932), Syria (1941), Jordan (1946), and Kuwait (1961). Therefore, none can boast historical claims to this or that border, other than the very ancient claims, including those of the Jews in the land of Israel with the Bible as their deed.

323

After World War I, the Turks were defeated and the British began to rule what was known as the British Mandate of Palestine, which lasted from 1917–1948.

British General Edmund Allenby addressing the people of Jerusalem at the Jaffa Gate.

This was the first time Christians had ruled Jerusalem since the days of the Crusaders. While there were three Jewish legions fighting with the British forces, the British were considered a Christian nation by the Muslims of the Middle East. The general that led the forces was General Edmund Allenby. As part of his campaign, leaflets were dropped by plane on the inhabitants of Jerusalem. These leaflets were printed in Arabic, telling them to surrender, and they were signed by General Allenby. In Arabic, his name could be misread as "Allah Nebi" which means "a prophet of Allah," putting great fear into the hearts of those who thought to defy this command.[13]

Allenby was a devout Christian and it is said he always kept the Bible at his bedside. Out of respect for the city, he dismounted his horse as he approached the Jaffa Gate, entered Jerusalem on foot, and declared "We have returned to you!" This was on December 11, 1917, and British rule lasted until 1948, when Israel became a sovereign nation.

At the beginning of British rule, there was   324
an effort to reinforce the national aspirations
of both the Arabs and Jews of the region. As
the Turkish Empire was being dissolved and
redivided among various ethnic groups, the horizon looked bright for the creation of a Jewish
state in the Middle East along with numerous
Arab Muslim states.

325   On October 31, 1917, the British War Cabi-
 net accepted the Balfour Declaration, which
was issued on November 2, 1917, as govern-
ment policy. It stated: "His Majesty's Government views with favour the establishment in
Palestine of a national home for the Jewish
people, and will use their best endeavours to
facilitate the achievement of this object, it
being clearly understood that nothing shall be done which may prejudice the civil and religious rights of existing non-Jewish communities in Palestine or the rights and political status enjoyed by Jews in any other country."

The Balfour Declaration was the result of   326
"circumstances" that brought the early Zionist
leader Dr. Chaim Weizmann, a British scientist,
into contact with the ex-prime minister of Britain, Arthur James Balfour. His scientific gifts
enabled him to render important services to
the admiralty and the Ministry of Munitions.
These gifts, including his invention of TNT,

*Map 8.
In 1919, all of
Palestine was
considered that
portion of the
Middle East
designated for the
Jewish people,
and included what
we know today
as Jordan, Israel,
and lands claimed
by the Palestinian
Authority.*

which helped win the war, brought him to the attention of Lloyd George, who became Minister of Munitions in the spring of 1915. All the while, Weizmann was spreading his message to all those who would give him an ear, of the need for a homeland in Palestine for the Jews. This included Balfour and Lloyd George.

In 1916, just before Britain conquered Palestine, there was a change of government in Britain, and Balfour became the foreign secretary and Lloyd George became the prime minister. Weizmann helped to draft the Balfour Declaration and it was accepted by the War Cabinet and became government policy.

Was this "circumstance" or was it God moving the hand of history to His prophetic end?

327

The Balfour Declaration won the approval of the United States and other Western powers. At first, there was hope that the Arabs would also accept it, as both the Arabs and the Jews were just breaking free from the yoke of the Ottoman Empire.

Emir Faisal, son of the acknowledged leader of the Arabs, Sherif Hussein, met with Dr. Chaim Weizmann and other Zionist leaders during the 1919 Paris Peace Conference. They signed an agreement by which the Arabs stated that "mindful of the racial kinship and racial bonds existing between the Arabs and the Jewish people" that "the surest means of working out the consummation of their [Jewish] national aspiration is through the closest possible collaboration of the development of the Arab state AND Palestine." (In 1919, Palestine was considered that portion of the Middle East designated for the Jewish people.) (See Map 8.)

328

The agreement between Faisal and Weizmann looked to the fulfillment of the Balfour Declaration and also called for "all necessary measures . . . to encourage and stimulate immigration of Jews into Palestine on a large scale, and as quickly as possible to settle Jewish immigrants upon the land through closer settlement and extensive cultivation of the soil."

329

On March 3, one day after Weizmann presented the Zionist case to the Peace Conference, Faisal wrote to Felix Frankfurter, a U.S. Supreme Court Justice and Zionist leader, declaring: "The Arabs, especially the educated among us, look with deepest sympathy on the Zionist movement. . . . We will wish the Jews a hearty welcome home. . . . We are working together for a reformed and revised Near East and our two movements complete one another. The Jewish movement is nationalist and not imperialist. Our movement is nationalist and not imperialist. And there is room in Syria for us both. [Under Turkish rule, Syria included part of Palestine.] Indeed, I think that neither can be a real success without the other."

Map 9.
In 1922, Palestine
was redivided as
Transjordan and
Palestine, giving
80 percent of the
Mandate to the
Arabs.

The British Mandate 1922

Faisal had conditioned his acceptance on 330
the fulfillment of British wartime promises to
the Arabs, who had hoped for independence in
a vast part of the Ottoman Empire.

These hopes were temporarily dashed when
the French took over the mandate for Syria,
ejecting Faisal from Damascus, where he had
been proclaimed king of Syria. As consola-
tion, the British named Faisal king of Iraq. In a further
effort to please the Arabs, British Colonial Secretary Win-
ston Churchill cut away 80 percent of the Jewish national
home in Palestine, some 35,000 square miles (90,565 sq.
km), and created a brand new Arab entity called Transjordan. Churchill installed Faisal's brother Abdullah as Emir.
(Abdullah is the great-grandfather of the present-day King
Abdullah II of Jordan.) Britain administered Transjordan
until 1946 when independence was granted and the name
of the area became the Hashemite Kingdom of Jordan (see
Map 9).

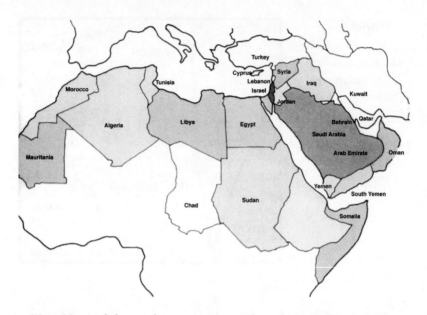

Map 10. Arab hopes for a vast empire have been realized. Today, the Arab League includes 21 separate Arab states spanning an area of more than 5,000,000 square miles. However, there is only one Jewish state, consisting of 8,000 square miles — Israel.

331  This apportionment — the first partition of Palestine and of the promised Jewish national home — was a blow to the Zionists. The Jewish people reluctantly accepted the partition because Britain simultaneously took over the League of Nations Mandate for Palestine in 1922, and they really had no one to whom they could appeal.

332

It should be emphasized that Arab hopes for a vast empire have since been realized. Today, the Arab League includes 21 separate Arab states spanning an area of more than 5,000,000 square miles (12.9 million sq. km). However, there is only *one* Jewish state consisting of 8,000 square miles (20,715 sq. km). It is called Israel (see Map 10).

333

While the Arabs showed early signs of acceptance of a Jewish state in Palestine in 1919, later it would be seen that once the Arabs had a taste of independent power they quickly lost interest in encouraging Jewish immigration and a Jewish state.

Nevertheless, the third *aliyah* (Jewish immigration movement) began in 1919, motivated by the Balfour Declaration and an open window of opportunity to bring oppressed Jews from eastern Europe and those fleeing communism which was taking control of Russia and surrounding nations. Over 50,000 Jews came home at this time. However, during the 1920s, the Arabs had a change of heart and attacks on the Jews of Palestine began in earnest. The fight was on from the Arab side to negate any hope of a Jewish state.

334

As time went on, the British feared their relations with the Arabs would suffer and sought to protect British oil interests in the Middle East. As World War II loomed on the horizon and oil became a paramount concern, British appeasement to the Arab cause against the Jews of Palestine was obvious. They greatly limited Jewish immigration in the British Mandate.

From 1936–1939, there was an Arab uprising in which 10,000 people were killed. The British showed leniency in the beginning, which resulted in a disaster — 1,000 British were killed, 500 Jews, and 8,500 Arabs (most of the Arabs were killed by other Arabs vying for control). In the end, the British had to use an iron-fist policy to stop the uprising. This put greater fear into the British, who put further limits on Jewish immigration. The climax was the British White Paper in 1939, which ordered that future Jewish immigration be limited to 10,000 per year for five years and to an additional 25,000 refugees from Nazism — 75,000 in all. Hardly much help while Hitler was killing 6,000,000 Jews during this same period.

At the end of a ten-year period, the White Paper called for an independent state in the region — an Arab state!

Haj Amin al-Husseini salutes Adolf Hitler in Germany.

During World War II, Haj Amin al-Husseini, the Muslim mufti of Jerusalem (uncle of the late Palestinian Authority Minister of Jerusalem Affairs, Faisal Husseini), met with Adolf Hitler to organize the extermination of the Jewish populations of the Middle East. Yasser Arafat was also related to this family by his mother.

335

As World War II came to an end, revealing the extent of the catastrophe that had befallen the Jewish people in Europe, there were demands everywhere for swift action to rehabilitate and resettle those who had survived the Holocaust, through the establishment of a Jewish state. The British had also tired of their role as supervisors of the British Mandate, which had been maintained since World War I. In Palestine, they were looking for a way out, as well as a way to appease both the Arabs and the Jews of this region.

336

The Holocaust, which claimed the lives of six million Jewish men, women, and children, one-third of world Jewry, had a severe impact on the Jewish people, which is still prevalent today. However, according to Ezekiel 37, the valley of dry bones, representing the "whole house of Israel," would

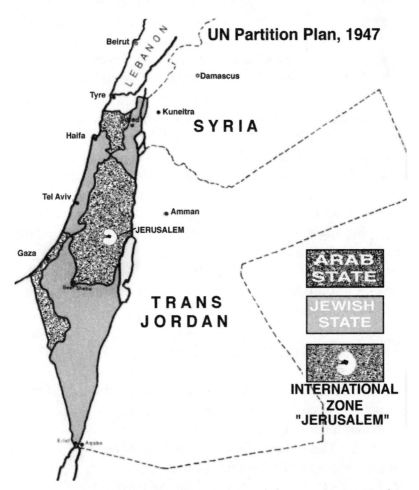

Map 11. The UN proposed a partition of the area into an Arab state and a Jewish state with Jerusalem an international zone. So, eager for independence, the Jews of Palestine were ready to accept a compromise — partition. But the Arabs boycotted the UN plan.

rise up out of their graves, come into their land of Israel, and become an "exceeding great army." This occurred in 1948 as a fulfillment of prophecy. God made it happen.

337   Prior to the founding of the state of Israel, the British tried, but failed, to work out an agreement acceptable to both Arabs and Jews on the issue of Palestine, so they turned the problem over to the United Nations early in 1947.

The UN sent an 11-nation Special Commission on Palestine (UNSCOP) to the region to investigate. UNSCOP found two people groups, Arabs and Jews, both claiming all the country. To satisfy the national aspirations of both peoples, UNSCOP proposed termination of the British Mandate and a partition of the area into an Arab state and a Jewish state based on population concentrations. Jerusalem would be an international zone.

The Jewish state was already in de facto existence in all areas. So, eager for independence, the Jews of Palestine were ready to accept a compromise — partition. The Arabs boycotted the UNSCOP plan. World opinion strongly favored the UN resolution, and it was adopted by a vote of 33–13, with 10 abstentions, on November 29, 1947.

Throughout the 1947 UN debate, the Palestine Arab Higher Commission threatened war, while Jewish Agency spokesmen appealed for peace. Jamal Husseini, spokesman for the Arab committee, told the UN on November 24, 1947, "The partition line proposed shall be nothing but a line of fire and blood."

338

Five days later, the UN voted for the partition and the Arabs began their war to prevent implementation of the UN resolution. Roads were mined, Jewish settlements isolated, and Jewish convoys were ambushed. By the end of that week, 105 Jews had been killed. Later, apartments in Jerusalem were blown up and more than 50 men, women, and children were killed. Thirty-five Hebrew University students were massacred on the road near Jerusalem. The Jewish Agency was bombed and took heavy casualties. A convoy was set afire on the road to Hadassah Hospital on Mount Scopus and 77 Jewish doctors, nurses, and scientists died.

339  On May 14, 1948, the state of Israel was declared to be independent and her Declaration of Independence was signed. Among its many clauses, it states:

"Eretz Israel (the land of Israel) was the birthplace of the Jewish people. Here, their spiritual, religious, and political identity was shaped. Here they first attained to statehood, created cultural values of national and universal significance, and gave to the world the eternal Book of Books. . . .

"Jews strove in every successive generation to re-establish themselves in their ancient homeland. . . . they made deserts bloom, revived the Hebrew language, built villages and towns, and created a thriving community, controlling its own economy and culture, loving peace but knowing how to defend itself. . . .

"The state of Israel . . . will foster the development of the country for the benefit of all its inhabitants; it will be based on freedom, justice, and peace as envisaged by the prophets of Israel; it will ensure complete equality of social and political rights to all its inhabitants irrespective of religion, race, or sex; it will guarantee freedom of religion, conscience, language, education, and culture; it will safeguard the Holy Places for all religions; and it will be faithful to the principles of the Charter of the United Nations.

"We extend our hand to all neighboring states and their peoples in an offer of peace and good neighborliness, and appeal to them to establish bonds of cooperation and mutual help with the sovereign Jewish people settled in its own land."

The flag of the state of Israel is based on the design of the Jewish prayer shawl (the tallit), represented in the two blue stripes on a field of white. The blue represents the Holy Spirit of God and the white represents heaven.

340

In the center, there is the Magen David, the Star of David, a symbol about which books have been written. One of the most meaningful interpretations of the Star of David comes from the noted Jewish scholar Franz Rosensweig. He sees the Star of David

as two triangles superimposed upon one another. One represents the nature of God, as Creator, Redeemer, and teacher. The other triangle represents the relationships between God, man, and others. Both of these interpretations are also consistent with a Christian understanding of the nature of God and man.

What a meaningful flag to have flying over a nation that is the fulfillment of Bible prophecy and the continuation of a covenant established by God with the Jewish people 4,000 years ago. This is a testimony to God's faithfulness to His people, His land, and His Word.

341

The Arabs rejected the partition and didn't accept their portion of land. Instead, five Arab armies (Egypt, Syria, Transjordan, Lebanon, and Iraq) immediately invaded Israel expecting to sweep the Israelis into the sea.

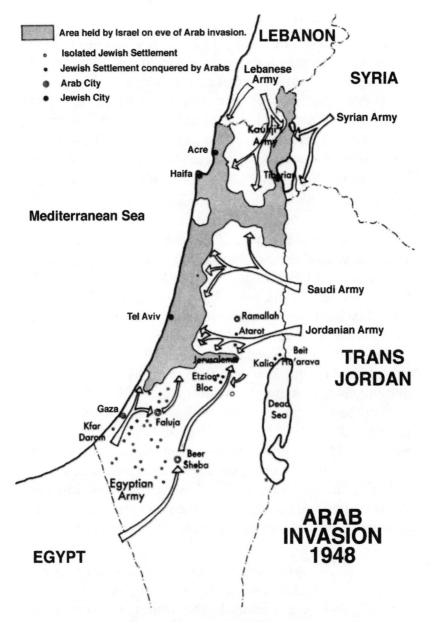

Map 12. In the Arab invasion of 1948, the Arab nations surrounding Israel sought to end all Jewish immigration and destroy the newly declared Jewish state of Israel.

On May 15, 1948, Azzam Pasha, secretary general of the Arab League, said in Cairo: "This will be a war of extermination and a momentous massacre which will be spoken of like the Mongolian massacres and the Crusades."

Fortunately, his words were not prophetic and Israel not only retained that which was given to her by the UN, but also a bit more. Those areas designated for the Arab state in Palestine were occupied by other Arab countries: the West Bank (of the Jordan River) by Jordan, and the Gaza Strip by Egypt.

342

After the establishment of the state of Israel, Jewish refugees of World War II and others from Muslim countries of the Middle East began to pour in. From 1948–1972, over 1,400,000 immigrants came into Israel. All had to be settled, trained, given Hebrew language classes, and many needed health care. All of this cost fell on the shoulders of the Israelis and the Jewish community worldwide.

For the Palestinian Arabs of Western Palestine, their rejection of the 1947 Partition Plan and their choice of war caused them to miss the first of many opportunities to obtain a national home — missed by their insistence on a policy of "all or nothing." The well-known Israeli diplomat Abba Eban often declared that "the Palestinians never miss an opportunity to miss an opportunity."

343

Arabs of the region also became refugees when they were encouraged to leave the area by the Arab leadership who intended to "push the Jews into the sea." However, even greatly under-armed and outnumbered, the Jews were not pushed into the sea and actually added land to their original allocation.

Refugees were created on both sides. However, an exchange of populations had actually taken place. By coincidence, the total number of Arabs who reportedly left Israel equaled the number of Jews who were forced out of the Arab countries.

There was also a more than even tradeoff of property between the Jews of the Middle East and the Arabs. The Jews who fled Arab countries where they had lived for 2,500 years left assets behind far greater than those the Arabs left in Israel. Jewish property that the Arabs confiscated in Iraq, Syria, Libya, and Egypt, more than offset Arab claims of compensation from Israel.[14]

After the war, in the negotiations for an armistice agreement in 1949, the Arabs, having lost, insisted that Israel then accept the 1947 partition lines as borders before they would negotiate. Actually, what they were demanding after defeat was what they could have had before their invasion without firing a shot! The purpose of this declaration by the Arabs was to appear as the defenders of the UN and its resolutions, and to cast Israel as its violator. The opposite was true.

This model created a novel concept, which the Arabs still use to this day: the doctrine of the limited liability war. Under this theory, an aggressor may reject a compromise settlement and may gamble on war to win everything in the comfortable knowledge that, even if he fails, he may insist on reinstating the original compromise and claim rights under it. This has been the pattern in each war of 1948, 1956, 1967, 1973, 1982, and even in recent declarations by the late Yasser Arafat, former head of the Palestinian Authority.

Map 13. In the armistice agreement in 1949, the Arabs demanded after defeat what they could have had before the invasion without firing a shot! The purpose of this declaration by the Arabs was to appear as the defenders of the UN and its resolutions, and to cast Israel as its violator. The opposite was true.

345

Currently, the Palestinians define "Palestine" as the region west of the Jordan River — that land comprised of Israel, the West Bank, and Gaza. However, according to the PLO Covenant, Palestine was defined as all of the land of Israel and Jordan.

The Arabs claim that Israel has usurped "all of Palestine," leaving the Palestinian people with nothing. This is simply not the case. Transjordan's independence, becoming Jordan in 1946, did force an artificial redefinition of "Palestine" to include only that area west of the Jordan River, thus restricting it to 20 percent of the original Palestine. What the 1947 UN partition did was to further partition the remaining 20 percent portion into yet another Arab state and a Jewish state. This, however, did not change the fact that Jordan is still part of historical Palestine, with over 70 percent of its population being Palestinian Arab. (Jordan's King Abdullah II is Saudi Arabian [father] and British [mother]; his great-grandfather having been given this territory by the British after World War I, which consisted of 80 percent of Palestine, and called the Emir of Jordan under British protection.)

With Jordan ignoring the UN partition and annexing the West Bank in 1949 (also known as Judea and Samaria), Palestinian Arabs under the Jordanian umbrella controlled 82.5 percent of the Palestine Mandate originally given to the Jews in 1917, while the Jewish State held a bare 17.5 percent (see Map 13).

Even today, Jordan is still a Palestinian Arab state in territory and by population, on 80 percent of the original Palestine of the British Mandate. A portion of the land apportioned by God to the tribes of Reuben, Gad, and Manasseh are also in Jordan, east of the Jordan River.

346

Despite what the Palestinians say, Israel did not usurp all of Palestine, nor are the Arabs left without a Palestinian state. All of Jordan is Palestine, too. The current peace process, from Oslo to the Wye River agreements, is seeking to find a nation for the Palestinians. However, only

Map 14. In the 1967 Six-Day War, Israel was attacked by Egypt and Jordan and won, defensively, the West Bank and Gaza. Jordan lost that war. Nevertheless, Jordan is still a Palestinian Arab state in territory and by population, on 80 percent of the original Palestine.

Israel is expected to give anything into this new state under the auspices of the Palestinians.

Jordan is giving nothing to the Palestinians. In fact, in Israel's peace treaty with Jordan, that country took land from Israel. Now, the Syrians are claiming the Golan Heights, which is home to 18,000 Israelis. This small region of 400 square miles (1035 sq. km) also provides one-third of Israel's water supply, and production from its bountiful agriculture and innovative light industry.

347  The use of the terms "Palestine" and "Palestinian," in association with the Arab population of the region, is a late phenomenon. It developed in the 1970s to give identity to a people who were a collection of Arab immigrants who came to the region in the past 100 years to find work, once the Jews started to arrive and improve the economy.

The noted Arab leader Auni Bey Abdul-Hadi told the Peel Commission (1936), "There is no such country [as Palestine]! Palestine is a term the Zionists invented! There is no Palestine in the Bible. Palestine is alien to us; it is the Zionists who introduced it."

The *Jerusalem Post* newspaper, founded in 1932, was called the *Palestine Post* and the Jews of the region were called Palestinians.

In 1946, Princeton professor Philip Hitti, a distinguished Arab historian testifying before the Anglo-American Committee of Inquiry, stated, "There is no such thing as Palestine in (Arab) history, absolutely not." He also opposed using the word "Palestine" on maps, because it was "associated in the mind of the average American, and perhaps the Englishman too, with the Jews."

The application of the term "Palestinian" to the Arab inhabitants of Palestine to the exclusion of Jews began to evolve in the early 1960s as the Arabs were trying to create a unified identity. However, neither the 1967 UN Security Council Resolution 242, nor the 1973 Resolution 338, mentioned Palestinians at all. It was only in the mid-seventies that the term first started being exploited by the PLO.

The Palestine Liberation Organization was **348** founded in May 1964 by the Arab League, having been promoted by Egyptian President Gamal Abdul Nasser. He saw it as a means to advance Egypt's goals of uniting the Arab world under Egyptian rule, by rallying the Arab states under the banner of destroying Israel. Since 1969, Yasser Arafat, the co-founder of the Fatah faction, headed up the PLO.

The PLO Covenant called for the destruction of Israel as well as Jordan, taking all of British Mandate Palestine as

*Emblem of the
Palestine Liberation
Organization (PLO)*

a Palestinian State. The Palestinian Authority has administered land and people in the West Bank and Gaza since they were turned over by Israel as part of the peace process. Arafat lived in Gaza from 1994 until his death in 2004.

Though the PLO/PA claims that it recognizes Israel's right to exist and wants to found a state only in Gaza and the West Bank, its official stationery betrays its true goals. The stationery, bearing its official emblem, shows all the land west of the Jordan River including all of Israel. These aims were part of the original charter and the organization's infamous Phased Program to gain the territory piece by piece until a pan-Arab war could be sparked for the final takeover of all of Israel.

Remember that the PLO was founded before the 1967 Six-Day War when Israel won the West Bank and Gaza from Jordanian and Egyptian sovereignty. Therefore, Arafat's claim to want only this small portion of his greater vision of all of Israel and Jordan rang hollow. The Arabs had this land before

1967, and still the organization was founded with its true aims of conquering all of Israel for Islam and the Arab world.

349   A final note on Palestine: Palestine was never a sovereign state (Arab or Jewish) that was somehow eclipsed in war, and thus needs to be reinstated back into the family of nations. What the Palestinians Arabs are asking for would be the creation of a completely new national entity that has never before existed.

Palestine was a regional name imposed on the area by the Roman emperor Hadrian, who came to quell the second Jewish revolt in A.D. 135.

Before the 1967 Six-Day War, Israel was constantly bombarded by artillery fire from Syria on the Golan Heights, and from terrorist raids from Syria, Egypt, and Jordan. There were massive military build-ups by the neighboring Arab states, especially Egypt. Egypt moved massive numbers of troops and equipment to the Israel-Egypt border in the Sinai, and ordered out the UN peacekeeping forces deployed there since the 1956 war with Egypt over the blockade of the Suez Canal. Egypt re-imposed the blockade of the Straits of Tiran in the Red Sea, effectively blocking Israeli shipping trade from the east via Eilat, and made a military alliance with Jordan.   350

At this point, Israel invoked its inherent right of self-defense and launched a pre-emptive strike on Egypt, destroying her air force before it left the ground. There were counterattacks from Egypt, Jordan, and Syria.

At the end of the Six-Day War, the previous cease-fire lines were replaced by new ones, with the West Bank (Judea and Samaria), Gaza, the Sinai peninsula, and the Golan Heights under Israeli control (see Map 14).

351   In 1973, on Yom Kippur (October 6), the Syrians and Egyptians coordinated a surprise attack against Israel. Yom Kippur is the holiest day on the Jewish calendar. It is a 25-hour period of total fasting from food and water, while praying at the synagogue to ask God to forgive one's sins. On this day, there is no work, no vehicles are on the roads, there is no television or radio, and no equipment operates.

The Egyptians crossed the Suez Canal, while the Syrian troops penetrated the Golan Heights. This lightning attack could have been fatal to Israel. However, God truly intervened. On the Golan Heights, Avigdor Kalahani, the commander of the tank corps, and one other tank managed to hold off the Syrian army until reinforcements could help.

During the next three weeks, the Israel Defense Forces turned the tide of battle and repulsed the attackers, crossing the Suez Canal into Egypt and advancing to within 20 miles (32 km) of the Syrian capital, Damascus. On October 22, the war was over.

In November 1977, the cycle of constant   352
Arab rejections of Israel's appeals for peace was broken with the visit of Egypt's President Anwar Sadat to Jerusalem. An accord was negotiated at Camp David in the USA in September 1978, and a formal peace treaty was signed on the lawn of the White House on March 26, 1979. This made Egypt the first

353   Arab country to accept Israel's hand that was extended in peace since 1948.

In 1980, a special law was enacted by the Knesset, the Israeli parliament, re-affirming that united Jerusalem is the capital of Israel.

Jerusalem has been the capital of no other nation or people in history except the Jewish people. Crown Prince Fahd of Saudi Arabia declared a *jihad* (a holy war) "to protect the Holy City against Zionist aggression."

In reaction to this declaration, foreign embassies in the city, including the U.S. embassy, moved to Tel Aviv. However, in 1990 the U.S. Congress affirmed the need to move the U.S. embassy from Tel Aviv to Jerusalem, which was ignored by successive U.S. presidents. So, on November 8, 1995, the U.S. Congress recognized united Jerusalem as the capital of Israel in the Jerusalem Embassy Act (public law 104-45), and demanded that the U.S. embassy be moved from Tel Aviv to Jerusalem. While the U.S. Senate almost unanimously voted for this move, all presidents since the vote have blocked the U.S. embassy move from occurring. Once the U.S. embassy moves, however, most other countries will follow suit.

Currently, U.S. citizens born in Jerusalem have no country ascribed to their place of birth. It only says, "Jerusalem" on their birth certificates, not "Jerusalem, Israel." The State Department needs to change their policy on this issue to comply with Congress.

For over a decade after the Palestinian Liberation Organization (PLO) had been forced out of Jordan by King Hussein in 1970, Israel underwent repeated shelling and terror attacks from PLO bases in Lebanon. The PLO had all but taken over parts of Lebanon, and their actions killed and wounded thousands of Israeli civilians who never knew when another attack was coming.

354

In June 1982, Israel launched the "Operation Peace for Galilee" campaign to rout the PLO out of Lebanon and bring peace and safety to her citizens.

In the first days of the war, approximately 100 Israeli U.S.-made jets faced off over Lebanon's Beka'a Valley with an equal number of Syrian, Russian-made MiGs. Israel also faced Syrian ground-to-air SAM missiles, which had taken a heavy toll on Israeli planes in 1973. At the end of one day, the Israel Air Force shot down 90 of the Syrian MiGs, while not one Israeli jet was lost. An Israeli government minister commented at the time that this had to be a miracle of God in the face of such odds. "Surely," he said, "Israel should have lost one plane due to mechanical or human failure." The operation achieved its objective within a few weeks, but a weak Lebanese central government kept Israeli troops there until 1985.

355  In December 1987, a Palestinian uprising called the *Intifada* erupted and swept throughout the Palestinian communities of the West Bank and Gaza. What had been a relatively benign relationship since 1967 between Israel and the Palestinians in the territories became a near war. Death and injuries on both sides were high, with great distress filling the hearts of Israelis and Palestinians alike. The *Intifada* continued for six years, until the current peace process began with the Oslo Accords in 1993.

In 1989, the Iron Curtain began to fall and Jews began to be liberated from the lands of the north — the provinces of the former Soviet Union where they had been prevented from immigrating to Israel for decades. Since that time, nearly one million new immigrants have arrived in Israel, including nearly 20,000 Ethiopian Jews from the lands of the south. Together, they fulfill Isaiah 43:5–6. 356

357   In 1991, the Gulf War, which was initiated to

restore sovereignty to Kuwait after it was invaded by Iraq, also affected Israel. Even though Israel was completely out of this war, 39 Scud missiles were fired upon Israel by Saddam Hussein's forces. He had hoped to draw Israel into the war because of his great hatred of her, but also to split up the allied coalition that not only had American and European forces, but participants from numerous Muslim Arab countries who have no ties with Israel.

During these dark days and weeks, fearing chemical and biological weapons, Israel prayed Psalm 91: "He who dwells in the shelter of the Most High will rest in the shadow of the Almighty. I will say of the LORD, 'He is my refuge and my fortress, my God, in whom I trust.' . . . He will cover you with his feathers, and under his wings you will find refuge; his faithfulness will be your shield and rampart. You will not fear the terror of night, nor the arrow that flies by day, nor the pestilence that stalks in the darkness, nor the plague that destroys at midday" (Ps. 91:1–6).

No chemical or biological weapons were used against Israel. Eleven thousand apartments were destroyed, but only one person died as a direct result of the destruction.

Truly, Israel was protected under the wings of the Lord, in whose shadow she dwells.

In 1992, the late Prime Minister Yitzhak   358
Rabin began negotiations with the Palestine
Liberation Organization (the PLO) in an effort
to make peace for Israel with the Palestinians

and other Arab nations. Only Egypt had signed a peace treaty with Israel in March 1979. Rabin and Arafat concluded an initial agreement in 1993, called the Oslo Accords, which was the first of many accords in the quest for peace in the region.

Map 15. As you can see, the geographical facts of relinquishing the West Bank and Gaza to the PA are astonishing, as it puts the terrorist enclaves in close proximity to Jewish population centers. The major cities of Israel then fall within range of the simplest hand-held rocket technology. At this point, Israel becomes almost indefensible.

To date, Israel has turned over all major centers in the West Bank (Judea and Samaria) and Gaza, while the Palestinians have done little to fulfill their side of the agreements.

359  In a violation of the Oslo Accords, Yasser Arafat declared over and over again his intentions to unilaterally declare a sovereign Palestinian state, with Jerusalem as its capital. He said he would raise the Palestinian flag on the walls of the Old City of Jerusalem and on the tops of the mosques and churches. In January 2000, Arafat declared, "This year is the year for declaring an independent Palestinian State. . . . It is a fundamental thing that this year is the year of the State." Israel has already made united Jerusalem its undivided capital and will not compromise on this. Therefore, if the Palestinians persist in pursuing his declared plan, then a conflict and even war is inevitable.

In 1994, Israel signed a peace treaty with the late King Hussein of Jordan. This has proved to be the warmest of the treaties, thus far. Considerable trade, tourism, and other bilateral initiatives have prospered both countries. 360

Today, "off and on" negotiations continue between Israel and Syria to hopefully secure a real peace with Syria and with Lebanon, which is controlled by Syria. The Syrian border has been quiet since 1973, but there are no relations between the countries and only a "cease-fire" exists.

361

 In May 2000, then Israeli Prime Minister Ehud Barak abruptly and unilaterally withdrew the Israel Defense Forces (IDF) from Lebanon, after an 18-year presence in a south Lebanon border buffer zone to thwart attacks from the

terrorist organization Hezbollah (Party of Allah). Hezbollah is a Shiite Muslim terrorist organization, headed by Sheik Hassan Nasrallah, with strong ties to Iran and Syria, and seeks to create a fundamentalist Islamic state in Lebanon, while attacking Israel with short- and medium-range missiles supplied by Iran and Syria. While Israel's move was praised by the world community as a step toward peace, Hezbollah saw this as a sign of victory for their tactics of firing missiles on Israel's northern cities and towns. Cross border attacks continued.

Subsequent to this, at Camp David (USA) **362** in July 2000, Israeli Prime Minister Ehud Barak offered generous terms to Yasser Arafat to get the stalled peace process with the Palestinians started again. He offered the Palestinians 93 percent of the West Bank and Gaza, three-fourths of the Old City of Jerusalem plus Arab neighborhoods, and a Palestinian Parliament building within eyesight of the Temple Mount, effectively making Jerusalem the capital of two states. However, Barak's desire to finalize an agreement and secure a fixed international border backfired when Yasser Arafat decided that the Hezbollah tactics just might work for the Palestinians. Arafat rejected Israel's offer, and on September 28, 2000, the Palestinians broke discussions with the Israelis and began a fierce war with Israel, known as the Second Intifada (Palestinian uprising or "shaking off") that has ebbed and flowed since then. Over 4,000 people have been killed on both sides, with many thousands more injured. During this period, grisly suicide attacks on Israeli civilian targets characterized the terror tactics used by several Palestinian terror groups, all sanctioned by the Palestinian Authority as legitimate. A true peace is certainly not on the Palestinian agenda, despite the efforts of Israel, and the quartet of the

USA, the European Union, Russia, and the United Nations to conclude a fair deal based on compromised and mutual recognition and bilateral support.

363 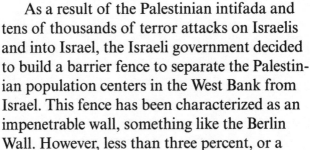 As a result of the Palestinian intifada and tens of thousands of terror attacks on Israelis and into Israel, the Israeli government decided to build a barrier fence to separate the Palestinian population centers in the West Bank from Israel. This fence has been characterized as an impenetrable wall, something like the Berlin Wall. However, less than three percent, or a mere 12.5 miles (20 km), of the eventual 447 miles (720 km) of fence is concrete wall. The rest is chain link fence with a dirt road on both sides to check for footprints, and electronic sensors to detect infiltration. The concrete sections are near Palestinian cities where taller buildings allow snipers to shoot at civilian drivers on nearby Israeli roads, and the wall blocks sniper fire. Yet the media constantly films and shows the same sections of concrete wall, and describes the fence as a wall, as though it were all concrete. The fence has 41 gates for farmers to tend their fields when the fence goes through their land. They have been entrusted with keys. There are 11 crossing points where people can move freely as long as they are not carrying weapons or explosives. Now that the Palestinians are using women and even small children, everyone is a potential bomb and must walk through metal detectors. There are five terminals for the transfer of goods between the PA and Israel.

The fence is located according to terrain and land use on both sides. Where Israel has crossed Palestinian farmland, the farmer has been compensated for the land, and given the value of five years of crop loss. In addition, Israel has transplanted over 63,000 olive trees to the Palestinian side of the fence so farmers will not lose access to their trees or income from oil production. Olive trees transplant easily without harm to the trees. Granted, there are some displacements of Palestinians; however, this is part of the unfortunate results of conflict.

Yasser Arafat died at a hospital in Paris, France, on November 11, 2004, at the age of 75. His second-in-command, Mahmoud Abbas (Abu Mazzen), became president of the Palestinian Authority. While Abbas projects a "grandfatherly" image in a business suit, he had been with Arafat since the 1950s and participated and even ordered numerous terrorist acts against Israel and other Western nations.

364

As a result of the inability of the Palestinian Authority to negotiate peace with Israel and suppress the rising power of Palestinian terror organizations, principally Hamas, the opportunity for a negotiated peace treaty became unattainable. Therefore, Israel, under Prime Minister Ariel Sharon and then Ehud Olmert, who became prime minister of Israel and head of Sharon's party, Kedema, developed a political plan for unilateral disengagement of Israel from the Palestinians to cut them off from their incessant war of attrition against Israel. In August 2005, Israel unilaterally pulled its citizens and the IDF out of Gaza, dislocating 8,000 faithful Israelis from 16 communities. Furthermore, these Jewish residents were a major agricultural producer using a unique hothouse system and ordinary beach sand to grow bountiful crops of vegetables and flowers, which also provided jobs for 4,000 Palestinians. Their agricultural output totaled $200 million per year, representing 15 percent of Israel agricultural output.

After the painful eviction of the Israelis, the Palestinians destroyed all of the Jewish communities in Gaza, instead of inhabiting these beautiful and well-kept towns and utilizing the greenhouses. Thus, the Palestinians also forfeited 4,000 jobs for Palestinians and the considerable income from which they could have benefited.

365  Despite Israel's effort to disengage from the Palestinians and make steps toward a peaceful disengagement and accept Palestinian statehood, in January 2006, the Palestinians elected the terror organization Hamas by a 56 percent margin (74 of 133 seats) as the ruling power in the Palestinian legislature. Ismail Haniya, a leader in the Hamas military wing, became the prime minister and refused to even recognize or speak to Israel. This rejection caused the nations of the world to boycott this new government until they recognize Israel, abide by previously negotiated agreements, and engage in further peace negotiations. On June 25, 2006, an Israeli soldier was kidnapped when the Palestinians tunneled a quarter mile (0.4 km) into Israeli territory and captured him while killing two other soldiers. Israel undertook a military operation to free the soldier and also acted to neutralize terror targets. Since the Gaza disengagement in August 2005, which left the Gaza Strip totally in Palestinian hands, the Palestinians had built and fired over 700 missiles into Israel. Instead of working to build a strong and positive Palestinian community, the PA and Hamas allowed, encouraged, and even participated in continued attacks on Israel. On July 10, 2006, the Hezbollah terror organization in Lebanon, headed by Sheik Hassan Nasrallah, attacked an Israeli army patrol, kidnapped two soldiers, and killed eight other people. This opened up a major escalation of the confrontation with both Hezbollah and Hamas in Lebanon and Gaza, as Hezbollah fired well over 1,000 short- and medium-range missiles (supplied by Iran and Syria) into Israel, hitting targets that have not seen such attacks in over 30 years.

Israel today is a modern-day miracle that has emerged because of hard work on the part of the Jewish people and God's prophetic blessing.

The only true democracy in the Middle East, Israel boasts a vibrant electoral system with dozens of political parties representing a variety of political views, from conservative to liberal Arab, secular to ultra-Orthodox Jewish.

Israel boasts an educational system that has given her citizens the highest literacy rate in the world and a medical system that provides guaranteed health care for all citizens and is sought after even by her enemies who arrive via neutral countries for treatment. She has a welfare system that provides goods and services to all in need — Jew and Arab alike — and an agricultural system that changed a barren, deforested land of desert and swamp into a lush and prosperous region that has made Israel one of the world's food exporting nations. She has an army which is a defense force that has been evaluated as the fourth most efficient army in the world.

Her main industries are still tourism and agriculture. However, high technology is now the largest revenue industry, creating everything from new computer designs and development of hardware and software to advanced medical and agricultural technology. Israel has now surpassed the Silicon Valley in the USA for high tech development.

The influx of immigrants into Israel from over 100 nations has given her a research and development (R&D) edge, since each nation has a different way of looking at a problem. With R&D teams made up of scientists and researchers from such varied locales as the former Soviet Union, the USA, India, South America, South Africa, and Europe all working on a problem, innovative products are being brought to the market almost daily.

Israel is known as an innovative nation. Just tell Israelis something can't be done, and they will figure out how to do it.

God is in control and His Word will be fulfilled regarding Israel, the Jewish people, His Church, and the anticipated soon arrival of the Messiah. As in the days of the Old Testament, even when it looks like all hope is lost and Israel will be vanquished, God has made a way, and shone forth His glory.

It is said of the Lord, "He who watches over Israel will neither slumber nor sleep" (Ps. 121:4). Let us be participants with God in this prophetic move. Let us pray for Israel and for the peace of Jerusalem. Only God's peace will be a lasting peace.

Let us also give gifts to help those returning to Zion and bless the restoration of the land of Israel. Let us volunteer our time, if we are able.

And let us travel to Zion ourselves to see what God is doing TODAY!

Endnotes

Chapter 1

1 Ruth Ward Heflin, *Jerusalem, Zion, Israel and the Nations* (Hagerstown, MD: The McDougal Publishing Co., 1994), p. 107–110.

2 Lance Lambert, *The Uniqueness of Israel* (Eastborne, UK: Kingsway Publications, Ltd., 1991), p. 15.

Chapter 2

1 Zev Vilnay, *The Guide to Israel* (Jerusalem, Israel: Daf-Cehn Press, Ltd., 1979), p. 320.

2 Flavius Josephus, *The Complete Works of Flavius Josephus, the Celebrated Jewish Historian* (Philadelphia, PA: Trans. W. Whiston, 1895), Wars IV, 8:4.

3 Israel Information Center, *Facts About Israel* (Rehovot, Israel: Atir, Ltd., 1992), p. 83.

4 Clarence H. Wagner Jr., *Lessons from the Land of the Bible* (Jerusalem, Israel: Bridges for Peace, 1998), p. 91.

5 Lambert, *The Uniqueness of Israel*, p. 15.

6 Vilnay, *The Guide to Israel*, p. 14.

7 Israel Information Center, *Facts About Israel*, p 78.

8 Ibid., p. 14.

9 Ibid., p. 16.

10 Ibid., p. 17.

11 Ibid.

12 Ibid., p. 19.

13 Ibid., p. 20.

14 Ibid.

15 Ibid., p. 21.

16 Ibid., p. 22.

17 Ibid., p. 26.

18 Ibid., p. 27.

Chapter 3

1 Heflin, *Jerusalem, Zion, Israel and the Nations*, p. 117–125.

Chapter 4

1 Eliyahu Tal, *Whose Jerusalem?* (Tel Aviv, Israel: The International Forum for a United Jerusalem, 1994), p. 12, 223–224.
2 Ibid., p. 123.
3 Teddy Kollek, from a speech given on August 11, 1988.
4 Ibid., p. 21.
5 Ibid., p. 184.
6 Ibid., p. 34.

Chapter 5

1 Mark Twain, *The Innocents Abroad* (Hartford, CT: The American Publishing Company, 1869), p. 486–487, 606.

Chapter 6

1 Dr. G. Douglas Young, *Young's Compact Dictionary* (Wheaton, IL: Tyndale House, 1989), p. 541.
2 Geoffrey Wigoder, *Almanac of the Bible* (New York, NY: Prentice Hall, 1991), p. 274.
3 *The NIV Study Bible* (Grand Rapids, MI: Zondervan Bible Publishers, 1985), Timeline Preface.
4 Israel Information Center, *Facts About Israel*, p. 15.
5 Ibid.
6 Ibid., p. 16.
7 Ibid.
8 Ibid., p. 21.
9 Ibid., p. 22.
10 Twain, *The Innocents Abroad*, p. 487.
11 A. Granott, *The Land System in Palestine: History and Structure* (London, 1952).
12 Moshe Aumann, *Land Ownership in Palestine: 1880-1948* (Jerusalem, Israel: Israel Academic Committee on the Middle East, 1976), p.14.
13 William L. Hull, *The Fall and Rise of Israel* (Grand Rapids, MI: Zondervan Publishing, 1954), p. 126.
14 Joan Peters, *From Time Immemorial* (New York, NY: Harper & Row, 1984), p. 25.

BIBLIOGRAPHY

Aumann, Moshe. *Land Ownership in Palestine: 1880-1948.*
Jerusalem, Israel: Israel Academic Committee on the Middle
East, 1976.

Bard, Mitchell G. and Joel Himelfarb. *Myths and Facts.*
Washington, DC: Near East Report,1992.

Bishko, Herbert. *This Is Jerusalem.* Tel Aviv, Israel: Heritage
Publishing, Ltd., 1973.

Duvernoy, Claude. *The Prince and the Prophet.* Jerusalem, Israel:
Christian Action for Israel, 1979.

Josephus, Flavius. *The Complete Works of Flavius Josephus, the
Celebrated Jewish Historian.* Philadelphia, PA: Trans. W.
Whiston, 1895.

Fleming, Dr. James. *The World of the Bible Gardens.* Jerusalem,
Israel: Biblical Resources, 1999.

Granott, A. *The Land System in Palestine: History and Structure.*
London, 1952.

Greenwood, Naftali. *Israel Yearbook and Almanac 1999.*
Jerusalem, Israel: IBRT Ltd., 1999.

Heflin, Ruth Ward. *Jerusalem, Zion, Israel and the Nations.*
Hagerstown, MD: The McDougal Publishing Co., 1994.

Hull, William L. *The Fall and Rise of Israel.* Grand Rapids, MI:
Zondervan Publishing, 1954.

Israel Information Center. *Facts About Israel.* Rehovot, Israel:
Atir, Ltd., 1992.

Israel Pocket Library. *History from 1880.* Jerusalem, Israel: Keter
Publishing House, Ltd., 1973.

Lambert, Lance. *The Uniqueness of Israel.* Eastborne, UK:
Kingsway Publications, Ltd., 1991.

The New International Study Bible. Grand Rapids, MI: The
Zondervan Corporation, 1985.

The New Scofield Reference Bible, Authorized King James
Version. New York: Oxford University Press, 1967.

Peters, Joan. *From Time Immemorial.* New York: Harper & Row,
1984.

Prince, Lydia. *Appointment in Jerusalem.* Waco, TX: Word Books,
1975.

Roth, C. and G. Wigoder, editors. *Encyclopedia Judaica.* Jerusalem, Israel: Keter Publishing House, Ltd., 1972.

Tal, Eliyahu. *Whose Jerusalem?* Tel Aviv, Israel: The International Forum for a United Jerusalem, 1994.

Twain, Mark. *The Innocents Abroad.* Hartford, CT: The American Publishing Company, 1869.

Vilnay, Zev. *The Guide to Israel.* Jeursalem, Israel: Daf-Cehn Press, Ltd., 1979.

Wagner, Clarence H. Jr. *Dispatch from Jerusalem.* Jerusalem, Israel: Bridges for Peace, 2nd quarter 1988.

Wagner, Clarence H. Jr. *Lessons from the Land of the Bible.* Jerusalem, Israel: Bridges for Peace, 1998.

Wigoder, Geoffrey. *Almanac of the Bible.* New York, NY: Prentice Hall, 1991.

Young, G. Douglas. *Young's Compact Bible Dictionary.* Wheaton, IL: Tyndale House Publishers, Inc., 1989.

About the Author

Clarence Wagner has lived in Israel for over 30 years, where he co-founded one of the leading international pro-Israel, evangelical Christian ministries headquartered in Jerusalem. His numerous books, articles, lectures, radio interviews, and television appearances bring current news and insights from Israel in light of Bible prophecy, as well as explore the biblical insights of our Christian faith from a Hebraic perspective.

Putting today's Christians into the context of life in Bible times, including today's events, reveals the deeper message of the Scriptures. Currently, he is the CEO of Genesis Strategic Solutions International, Ltd., which brings Christian investment and business partnerships to the Israeli marketplace, boosting the economy and providing jobs to Israelis and new immigrants as they return to their ancient homeland in fulfillment of Bible prophecy.

Other books by Clarence Wagner include *Where Was Love and Mercy?* and *Lessons from the Land of the Bible.*

He can be contacted at gssi_itd@hotmail.com